PREDICT THE NEXT
BULL
OR BEAR
MARKET
AND WIN

How to Use Key Indicators to Profit in Any Market

PREDICT THE NEXT

BULL

OR

BEAR

MARKET

AND WIN

Michael Sincere, author of the bestselling
Understanding Options and *All About Market Indicators*

Avon, Massachusetts

Published by
Adams Media, a division of F+W Media, Inc.
57 Littlefield Street, Avon, MA 02322. U.S.A.
www.adamsmedia.com

ISBN 10: 1-4405-7171-6
ISBN 13: 978-1-4405-7171-8
eISBN 10: 1-4405-7172-4
eISBN 13: 978-1-4405-7172-5

Printed in the United States of America.

10   9   8   7   6   5   4   3   2   1

Library of Congress Cataloging-in-Publication Data

Sincere, Michael.
Predict the next bull or bear market and win / Michael Sincere.
pages cm
Includes index.
ISBN 978-1-4405-7171-8 (pb) -- ISBN 1-4405-7171-6 (pb) -- ISBN 978-1-
4405-7172-5 (ebook) -- ISBN 1-4405-7172-4 (ebook)
1. Stock price forecasting. 2. Stock exchanges. I. Title.
HG4637.S563 2014
332.63'222--dc23
                                          2013051348

Cover design by Sylvia McArdle.

This book is available at quantity discounts for bulk purchases.
For information, please call 1-800-289-0963.

Dedication

To my mother, Lois, whom I will always remember for her compassion and generosity, who asked for so little while accomplishing so much; and to my father, Charles, for his kindness and positive attitude.

Contents

Introduction

This book, written for beginners and beyond, is about making profits as well as limiting risk. I will show you strategies that will help you to prosper during bull markets, be cautious during sideways markets, and avoid bear markets altogether (although I will also show you how to make a profit when the market is going down).

Although your ultimate goal is to use the stock market to build wealth, you must also avoid losing money. By studying the overall market, you can go along for the ride when times are good (bull market), but avoid getting hurt when times are bad (bear market).

Unfortunately, many people buy stocks when the market has reached a tipping point and is about to plunge. Others sell all their stocks after the market has already hit bottom. This book will help you to avoid making these common mistakes.

In addition, if you are too emotional about the overall stock market, you will be either irrationally exuberant during bull markets or overly pessimistic during bear markets. One can lead to disaster, and the other to missed opportunities. This book will help you find that healthy balance, which comes from being an astute market observer.

Too many people underestimate the importance of observing the overall market when entering the stock market. If you step into the market without studying market conditions, it's similar to being on a boat in the middle of the ocean without checking whether a threatening storm is headed your way or if it will be sunny with blue skies. So before you step into that ocean we call the stock market, you need to determine if it's safe.

Surprise!

In this book, you'll also find a few surprises. For example, no one can *consistently* predict what the market will do tomorrow, next week, or next year. It would be nice if this were possible, but since the market was first created, few have made market predictions that were correct all of the time—or even most of the time.

Many people try. Every day, people make forecasts, some of them quite dramatic, and most of the time, they're wrong. When the market is climbing higher, you may see an article titled "The Market Will Crash Next Week!" These dramatic headlines do little but scare investors into selling their stocks, usually at the wrong time.

It's even more common to read extremely upbeat predictions that the market is going to rise by 10, 20, or 30 percent this year or the next. On financial television programs, and in newspaper articles, the message given to investors is that the market will almost always go up. One guy on a financial program even claims, "There's always a bull market somewhere!" (That means, presumably, that there must always be a bear market somewhere, too.)

Let me be clear up front what I can and cannot do: I cannot teach you to consistently predict what the market is going to do next. Using the methods in this book, you will get it right part of the time but not always. That's the bad news.

The good news is that after reading this book, you will know how to use clues, indicators, and observation to read the market. If you can correctly interpret that information, you can stay invested in bull markets and avoid bear markets. You will not always be right, but if you can be right more times than not, you're on your way to success.

Everyone wants to beat the market; but rather than trying to beat the market, why not follow the market when it's going up, and avoid it before it goes down? The smart money does not come from catching every top or bottom. Instead, it comes from being on the right side of the market for the majority of the biggest moves.

Many people say that's impossible. I disagree. I think it is possible to read the market. By using a handful of indicators, your own observations, and market clues, you can prosper in bull markets while protecting your assets during bear markets. Not only do I believe it's possible but I did it, and so have others that I know. (You can also see how I'm doing by reading my weekly blog at *www.michaelsincere.com*, where I analyze the market using the tactics and tools included in this book.)

One of the reasons you're reading this is so you can do your own analysis. Although no one has a crystal ball, nevertheless, using clues and tools, it is possible to put the probabilities on your side. If you can be 55 percent correct, you can do well in the market (but there are never any guarantees).

Jesse Livermore, one of the greatest stock speculators in history, discovered the importance of looking at the big picture. He said that his strongest allies in the market are underlying conditions, and as long as you don't get impatient, they are the most dependable method of making big money. In this book, you will learn not only how to examine underlying market conditions but also how to trade the overall market. By being able to anticipate the direction of the underlying market, you have a better chance of success.

Market Mastery

When we talk about the "market," it typically means the Dow Jones Industrial Average, the Standard & Poor's (S&P) 500, the Nasdaq, or the Russell 2000. These are all indexes. Most people think of the market as the Dow Jones since each day the media reports on the change in the thirty stocks included in the Dow. The S&P 500, however, includes 500 large U.S. stocks, and represents the entire U.S. stock market, not just thirty stocks.

If you are confused by some of the vocabulary in this book, I recommend that you read my book *Understanding Stocks* (McGraw-Hill, 2nd edition). This book, written for beginners, will introduce you to the stock market. It discusses investment and trading strategies, and also introduces you to options, bonds, mutual funds, index funds, and commodities. Obviously, there are many other books about the stock market as well.

There are several ways to participate in the market. For example, you can buy individual stocks, exchange-traded funds (ETFs), or mutual funds. If you want to buy market indexes, you can buy ETFs that track the major market indexes or buy index mutual funds (these investments will be discussed later). Also, if you are one of the millions of investors who have a 401(k) or IRA, you will be able to use almost all of the strategies included in this book.

Now, let's get started.

CHAPTER 1

Study Underlying Market Conditions

So many people are focused on the performance of individual stocks that they don't take the time to look at what the overall market is doing. Knowing how to read the market as a whole will help you to prosper during bull markets and protect assets during bear markets.

Often investors do the opposite. They blindly gorge on stocks at the end of a bull market while avoiding the market after it has already hit bottom. If they had taken the time to study the overall market, this might have helped them make better decisions. Imagine being lost in a forest with only a candle. It would be difficult to find your way. If you had better tools such as a GPS, a compass, and a flashlight, it would be much easier to navigate out of the forest. Many of the tools you will read about in this book are similar to a GPS—they'll show you the best path to follow.

If you are a beginner, it's important to be aware of underlying market conditions. It is one of the keys to your success as an investor or trader. You will learn how to use clues and tools (i.e., indicators) for guidance. Although there are no guarantees that you will leave the forest unharmed, the probabilities of that happening are higher if you have the right equipment.

Put the Probabilities on Your Side

Jesse Livermore, a trader and author, was the first to discover that to make big money, he had to correctly appraise overall market conditions. He considered it one of his most important discoveries.

In the early 1900s, Livermore was surprised that not even a world war could stop the market from being a bull market. To make money, he said, all a trader needs to know is how to appraise conditions. Livermore used to visit a particular bucket shop (this was similar to a brokerage firm but with fewer regulations). Every time Livermore was there, someone would ask one of the regular customers, Mr. Partridge, what he thought of the market. Mr. Partridge would always give the same answer: "It's a bull market!" At first, Livermore thought it was funny, but then he made another discovery (which is introduced in the thinly disguised biography about his trading experiences, *Reminiscences of a Stock Operator*, written by Edwin Lefevre).

"I think it was a long step forward in my trading education when I realized at last that when old Mr. Partridge kept on telling the other customers, 'Well, you know this is a bull market!' he really meant to tell them that the big money was not in the individual fluctuations but in the main movements—that is, not in reading the tape but in sizing up the entire market and its trend."

In other words, if you want to make big money, you must learn how to assess the entire market. Is it easy? No. Is it possible? Yes. By learning how to read the market, you can put the probabilities for success on your side.

There are many other strategies to employ, which we'll get to later. Basically, it's a lot easier to buy when the market is strong and moving higher, and sell before the market goes down. Sound like common sense? It is.

Even more important, if you learn how to read the market yourself, you don't have to depend on acquaintances, neighbors, know-it-all TV commentators, or authors to tell you what to do. Instead, you can rely on your own knowledge, clues, and most important, market indicators.

By learning how to uncover some of those clues, it will be easier to understand the market. There are no magic tricks that will offer instant enlightenment, but if you can learn to look for those clues, then you will be in a good position to profit.

Be a Market Observer

As mentioned previously, one of the most important skills you can develop is to be an astute market observer. By learning how to observe the market, you will gain an edge over other investors and traders, many of whom ignore overall market conditions. By watching the market carefully, you will be more aware of economic changes, world events that affect the market, trend changes, or when a bull or bear market is beginning or ending.

Legendary fund manager Peter Lynch used to go to various companies—in malls, car dealerships, or wherever there were shoppers—to observe whether people were buying its products, and to see which stores at the mall were the most popular. That was how he got some of his best stock ideas. You can use the same skills with the stock market.

Be a Stock Detective

In many ways, to successfully figure out the market, you have to be a stock detective. As in the best mystery stories, when you look for clues there will be many red herrings, wrong turns, and false leads. Even worse, there are many people who will use the media to try to mislead you.

As a stock detective, however, you have to figure out what information is real and what is just hype. It would be nice if this were easy but it's not. When you participate in the stock market, you enter a very strange world where the rules are different, where logic doesn't always matter.

Whether you buy individual stocks or index funds, it is a lot easier to earn money when the power of a bull market is behind you. In a bull market, the wind is at your back and you can sail across the ocean with ease. It's a lot easier to sail, or invest, when the market is carrying you along.

If you can determine that overall market conditions are changing, and a bear market is near, you will want to protect yourself. Being in a bear market is similar to getting caught in the middle of the ocean with lightning, rain, and fog, when the wind is blowing right in your face.

Bottom Line

Follow the market and the market trend.

Is This Market Timing?

Some of you might think that avoiding bear markets sounds suspiciously like the strategy of market timing. Perhaps you heard that market timing doesn't work. It's true that it's extremely difficult to consistently time the market. In fact, timing the market each day or week is primarily for short-term traders.

On the other hand, if you can stay in the market during the majority of a bull market and avoid or reduce exposure in bear markets, that's being smart. Reducing or limiting risk makes sense.

It's also true that people are slow to react to market conditions. Most investors, including some pros, do not get out of bear markets in time and are also slow to enter bull markets. It's human nature.

Because of our emotions, we tend to do what feels right, but it may not be the right strategy.

As you'll learn later, when the market is soaring so high it appears as if the stock market is giving away free money, you should be cautious. While other investors are gobbling up stocks and making money, you are slowly selling. Although you will never time it perfectly, by observing the overall market as well as investor behavior, you will learn to recognize some of the warning signs of an impending bear market. (Note: A red warning light should flash for you when it's too easy to make money in the market.)

Conversely, during those times when investors are frightened of the market and are panic selling, you will be looking to buy. Although it's rare for you to catch the exact low of the market, one of your goals is to determine when it's safe to buy again. The only way to know is by evaluating underlying market conditions.

In the next chapter we'll look at the characteristics of a bull market—that is, when the market generally goes up.

CHAPTER 2

Characteristics of a Bull Market

In this chapter, you will learn how a bull market starts and develops, the clues and signals that tell you how long it will continue, and the signs that it is ultimately coming to an end.

Bull Market: When Wall Street Throws a Party

Bull markets are profitable for nearly everyone. Brokerage firms are pleased because investors are putting more money into the market and generating commission dollars for the brokers. Money managers are pleased because they earn substantial returns and receive huge end-of-year bonuses.

Wall Street firms hire more employees to handle the new accounts, and underwriters launch new initial public offerings (IPOs). Individual investors are delighted because the value of their 401(k)s and IRAs rise, which makes them feel wealthier. Businesses are happy because consumers spend more money, boosting the economy. It seems as if every investment strategy works, from buy-and-hold to short-term trading.

During a bull market, almost everyone is in a stock-buying mood, often for no reason except that everyone else is buying. During these times, the major indexes (as well as most individual stocks) go up, sometimes dramatically.

Overall, investors are optimistic about their personal finances, and if the bull market goes high enough, some will brag about how much money they're making. When the stock board has turned to green (it's red in down markets), it seems that no matter which stock you buy, it's going up.

During a bull market, if you invest in an index ETF or index mutual fund that mimics the major market indexes such as the S&P 500 or Dow 30, you can make money, sometimes lots of money. If you look at a stock chart of a trending market, you will see that the trend is pointing in one direction: up (for bull markets).

Market Mastery

Exchange-traded funds are designed to track a specific market index. The index ETFs discussed in this book track the major, broad-based market indexes such as S&P 500 (SPY), Dow Jones Industrial Average (DIA), Nasdaq-100 (QQQ), and Russell 2000 (IWM).

Although the market doesn't rally every day, selloffs don't last long in a bull market. In fact, when there is a selloff, those connected to the financial markets say that it is a "healthy" pullback, an opportunity to buy at bargain prices. They suggest that the "market needs time to digest its gains."

During a bull market, there is usually positive news on TV and in the newspapers. Negative news (such as that a company has an earnings miss) is forgotten by the next day. The higher the market goes, the more enthusiastic people get about the market. Those who work and play on Wall Street are in a party mood because their livelihood depends on the market going higher.

Perhaps the only people who despise bull markets are short-sellers, that is, people who make money when the market goes down.

How Does a Bull Market Start?

Not every bull market is the same. For example, some bull markets are exciting and fun, while others move up so slowly it's barely noticeable. The market rises on the hope and enthusiasm that the economy will continue to get better. This optimism could be in response to a new technology, a housing boom, or the Federal Reserve (the Fed) keeping interest rates low. Whatever the reason, the market goes higher.

To follow the path of a bull market, you must look at what came before. More than likely, before the bull market started there was a bear or sideways market. After a bear market, the market often goes sideways for a long time; it could take months or years before it comes back to its previous high. (I consider a sideways market to be one in which no new multi-month highs or lows are made and *support* and *resistance* levels are not broken. You will learn about support and resistance levels later.)

Therefore, giving a single answer to the question "How does a bull market start?" is impossible. What we can say is that in every big decline eventually there is a bottom, after which the market starts to recover, or at least does not sink further. Unfortunately, no one knows that the market has reached bottom until after it's already done so.

For example, most people believe that the October 1929 stock market crash was the bottom. In fact, the market made many attempts to rally, but for three years, every rally failed. After those three years, when the market finally stopped falling, many people weren't willing to invest in the market again. Mark Twain's quip represented the common feeling about the stock market: "I'm not as concerned about the return *on* my money as I am the return *of* my money."

After the market hits bottom, there's so much pessimism remaining from the bear market that many investors are reluctant to participate in the market. The only people still in the market are those who bought and held on the way down, a few brave investors, or short-term traders. Those who lost most or all of their money don't believe there will ever again be a bull market. Thus, at the start of many bull markets most investors are suspicious and unwilling to participate. They want to avoid the pain of more losses.

Typically, after a decline the market goes sideways for a long while. From the ashes of the bear market, the market moves up once again . . . eventually. It can take years of a rising market, with many fits and starts along the way, before people realize, "Hey, it's a bull market!"

Investors go through a predictable cycle of emotions ranging from despair (bear market) to euphoria (bull market). If you can identify which stage most investors are at and how they're feeling, you should do the opposite. As mentioned earlier, most investors do what feels right emotionally, and that is usually the wrong move.

Following is a chart of the range of feelings that investors feel during a typical bull and bear market cycle. This chart will help you to plan future strategies. (Later, we'll discuss many different strategies you can use in any market environment.)

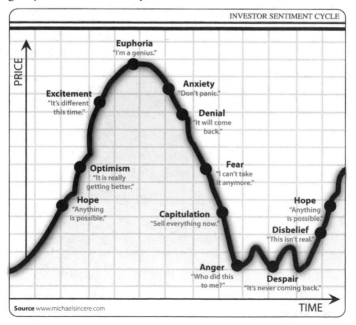

INVESTOR SENTIMENT CYCLE

PRICE

Euphoria
"I'm a genius."

Anxiety
"Don't panic."

Excitement
"It's different this time."

Denial
"It will come back."

Optimism
"It is really getting better."

Fear
"I can't take it anymore."

Hope
"Anything is possible."

Hope
"Anything is possible."

Capitulation
"Sell everything now."

Disbelief
"This isn't real."

Anger
"Who did this to me?"

Despair
"It's never coming back."

Source www.michaelsincere.com

TIME

Getting Back to Even Isn't Good Enough

After losing money in a bear market, many people would be happy just to get their accounts back to their previous highs. Fortunately for them, bear markets eventually end and new bull markets appear.

Remember, in the early stages of a bull market, there are few believers. Because the wounds from the previous bear market are still fresh, many investors warn others to stay away from the market. No one wants to get burned a second time, so the warnings simply exaggerate the fears.

If you look at sentiment readings from the American Association of Individual Investors (AAII), for example, bearish levels may be as high as 65 or 70 percent.

Each week, AAII, a nonprofit educational organization, polls its members for their view of the market: bullish, bearish, or neutral (the survey results are published at *www.aaii.com/sentimentsurvey*). AAII can be surprisingly accurate, and it's a useful guide— as long as you do the opposite of what the members are feeling (it's a contrarian indicator). Therefore, when AAII members are over 65 percent bearish, that is a bullish signal. Conversely, when AAII members are over 65 percent bullish, that is a bearish signal. Although these surveys measure extreme emotions, don't use them to time the market. After all, investors can remain overly bullish or bearish for long periods. Nevertheless, AAII can give important insights into the current investor's mood.

Another sentiment survey, Investors Intelligence, published by Chartcraft, polls more than 100 independent financial newsletter writers for their view of the market. Again, this is a contrarian indicator: If the newsletter writers are 65 or 70 percent bullish, it is a bearish signal. If they are 65 to 70 percent bearish, it is a bullish signal. At market extremes, this survey is also remarkably accurate. You can find Investors Intelligence at *www.investorsintelligence.com* (subscription required).

Market Mastery
AAII and Investors Intelligence survey results can also be found on my weekly blog at *www.michaelsincere.com*.

Once the market gets past the anger, fear, and warnings of further declines, it often moves higher (which is why it's important to monitor sentiment indicators). Bad news around the world or a poor economy and extreme pessimism may linger, but sooner or later a new bull market begins.

It's a Bull Market!

The good news about bull markets is they often last a long time, usually for years. So even if you're late to the party, you may still have time to partake of milk and cookies for a while. The bad news is that it takes time to know if what you're seeing is a new bull market or just a bear market rally.

Note: Unlike bull markets, which may last for one to seven years, bear markets tend to be shorter, lasting a few months to a year.

When Anything Is Possible

Although the length of bull markets can vary, it's important to remember this: The stock market can go higher (or lower) than anyone ever thought possible. A lot depends on how the bull market started, the conditions that made it possible, and whether those conditions still exist.

No one rings a bell when a bull market starts. More than likely, you will get many mixed messages at the beginning. People you respect will warn you to stay away from the market, while strangers may predict that stocks are going to the moon. It's hard to know whom to believe. The answer, of course, is to believe no one. Rely on your own analysis and insights.

The Chart Reveals the Truth

It doesn't matter whether you're an investor or trader—by pulling out a chart of the major market indexes, you can discover important clues. If you know nothing about charts, you can read my book *Understanding Stocks*, or look on your brokerage firm's website. A number of websites have good charting software, including Google Finance, Yahoo! Finance, or Stockcharts.com, to name a few.

There is no better way to identify an uptrend (i.e., bull market) than by looking at a chart. Although using fundamental analysis can help when looking at individual stocks, when looking at the overall market, I highly recommend that you rely on charts. Charts display a variety of technical data (i.e., technical analysis) such as *support and resistance, overbought* and *oversold* conditions, stock patterns, and trends. By reading a chart, you will get clues as to underlying market conditions as well as whether your stock or index is in an *uptrend* or *downtrend*.

During a bull market, if you look at a three-month, six-month, or one-year chart of the S&P, Dow, or Nasdaq during a bull market, you will see that stock prices are pointing up—that is, it's an uptrend. Of course, even during a bull market there will be pullbacks that last a few days, or perhaps a few weeks. However, the overall trend of the market will be higher.

Sometimes those pullbacks are sharp, perhaps 5 to 10 percent off the recent highs. This is a normal occurrence. If the market continues to go higher after the pullback, more than likely the structure of the bull market remains intact.

What about the P/E Ratio?

One fundamental indicator that can be helpful when analyzing the state of the market is the *price to earnings (P/E) ratio*. This is the stock's current price divided by earnings per share for the previous twelve months. Traditionally, the average P/E of the S&P 500 is 15, so if you look at the P/E of the entire market and it's lower, then the market may have room to go higher. If the P/E of the entire market is higher than 15, it's possible that the bull market is in its later stages.

Market Mastery

Don't rely only on a high or low P/E to determine whether it's a bull or bear market. One of the problems with the P/E ratio is that during extreme markets, it's not that effective an indicator. After all, the P/E can remain high for long time periods during bull markets. Still, it's a good idea to compare the current P/E with its historical norm.

Economic Indicators Give Buy Signals

As the market climbs higher, some of the economic indicators may start to turn upward. Keep in mind—and this is important—the economy may *not* appear to be in recovery mode at first, especially during the early stages of a bull market. In fact, many economic signs may still be poor, which is why many people are surprised when the market moves higher. Often the market moves higher just on the expectation that the economy will improve. In other words, the market is leading the recovery.

During a bull market, economic conditions may be dismal and political conditions unsettled (or worse) but the market keeps going higher. That is the power of a bull market, and you shouldn't fight the uptrend. If you are overly worried, pull some money off the table for diversification; i.e., put it into cash. But do not exit a bull market without a solid reason—pay attention to your clues and indicators.

During a bull market, another factor at play is the actions of the Federal Reserve System (the Fed), which is the central banking system of the United States. In reality, it's the actions of the twelve-member FOMC (Federal Open Market Committee) that receives all the media attention and that people watch closely. This policy-making committee has the power to raise or lower interest rates, which affects the bond market, as well as the stock market. For example, from 2008 to 2013, in response to a financial crisis, the Fed kept interest rates artificially low by buying billions of dollars in bonds. That helped fuel one of the strongest bull markets in history.

The bond-buying program, *quantitative easing* (QE), was cooked up by the Fed to help the economy in the wake of the 2008 recession. This program, in turn, lit up the stock market. As an astute market observer, you should pay attention to what the Fed is or is not doing. It has tremendous influence over the economy, including the stock market.

Don't Fight the Fed

With the ability to raise or lower interest rates, the Fed can send the markets climbing to dizzying heights or crashing into the ground. The market is pleased by accommodating Fed policies (when the Fed lowers interest rates or increases stimulus) and is displeased if the Fed is not so friendly (when it raises interest rates or reduces stimulus).

No matter how bad the economy appears, if the Fed is lowering interest rates by buying billions of dollars in bonds (or using other tools), the market will likely rise. Therefore, if you try to fight the Fed by betting against the market, you'll probably lose the battle.

When the Fed releases its minutes, or if the Fed chairperson makes an unexpected comment, the market may react strongly. The Fed uses a number of tools to meet its financial goals, such as keeping inflation low and employment high, so the chances are usually good that it will say positive things about the economy.

Market Mastery

If you are a short-term trader (rather than a long-term investor), you can take advantage of the extreme volatility that occurs after a Fed meeting, especially if the Fed unexpectedly changes interest rates. If there is a major market selloff, the Fed may try to stop the carnage by lowering interest rates or use other tools to stop the bleeding.

The Fed is not perfect, and there are times when it makes the wrong move. When the Fed can't help the market (or perhaps makes things worse), the financial markets react strongly (to put it mildly; usually all hell breaks loose). Fortunately, the Fed doesn't do this too often, and many of its mistakes—when it makes them—aren't readily apparent.

Bottom Line

Always observe the actions of the Fed and the economy to determine the best place to invest your money. If the Fed doesn't get it right, the bull market may end abruptly. That is why you should pay attention to what the Fed does or doesn't do. Its actions have immediate effects on the economy, and on the stock market. When the Fed speaks, the market listens and reacts.

Economic Indicators

In addition to the P/E ratio and the actions of the Fed, there are a handful of economic indicators that you should keep your eye on. It's not so much what data they show, but the reaction of the market to the data. Here are a few of the most important economic indicators that can move the market:

1. Interest Rates

It's always a good idea to watch interest rates, especially the 10-year Treasury, which is expressed as a percentage. To be precise, it's the Chicago Board Options Exchange (CBOE) Interest Rate 10-year Treasury Note (Symbol: ^TNX).

If the yield on the 10-year Treasury moves up, especially if it spikes, that will cause bond prices to fall and probably disrupt the stock market. Conversely, if the yield on the 10-year Treasury moves down, then bonds will rise in price, and the stock market may also rise (because it likes low-interest-rate environments).

However, because economic conditions are unpredictable, it's difficult to make hard and fast rules about what you should and shouldn't do when the yield rises or falls. The best advice is to be flexible and to react as conditions change. Because the economy changes slowly, you have time to adjust your portfolio. If the yield on the 10-year Treasury continues to spike higher, however, consider selling any bond mutual funds.

2. Inflation

The Consumer Price Index (CPI) is an indicator that measures the change in prices over a given period. Simply put, the CPI survey helps to measure inflation. Unfortunately, inflation is one of those economic conditions that can creep up on you. Like frogs being boiled in a pot of water, by the time people realize that inflation is heating up and interest rates are rising, the economic damage has already been done.

As a market observer, always be aware of inflation (or deflation, but that is relatively rare). If it increases, that could be a signal to cut back on stocks, though that shouldn't be the only factor in your decision.

3. The Monthly Jobs Report

When the jobs report is released each month, the market may have a strong reaction to the data. In the wacky world of Wall Street, analysts may view an overly strong jobs number as negative because interest rates might rise. Conversely, if the jobs number is weak, then the market might rally (at least for a day), because interest rates will remain low.

Usually, as the market goes higher, the economic data support the bullish market conditions. At times, however, the market separates itself from the real economy and goes in a different direction (either much higher or lower). If that happens, it is a clue that the market is out of step with reality. Take that as an indicator of probable future market performance. For example, if the market is rising steadily higher even though economic data are negative, it's likely that the market will eventually come back to earth sooner rather than later. However, don't take this statement to the bank. We also know that bull and bear markets can extend far longer than any reasonable person can anticipate.

The Bull Market Gets Stronger

As the bull market continues, some investors, nervous about the preceding bear market, will be slow to recognize that a new bull market has already begun.

If you are *long* the market (i.e., you bought stocks, mutual funds, or ETFs and will profit when the market goes up), then you are pleased because you are making money. As the market goes higher, enthusiasm for the market gets stronger. On the other hand, as the market rises, many contrarian investors (including some financial columnists and perhaps your acquaintances) deny it's still a bull market. They warn that the market has gone too high. As the bull market climbs, many more will predict that the market is going to crash.

Financial columnists love to make crash predictions. After all, if they are right, they will get a lot of good publicity and bragging rights for many years. In truth, if they predict it often enough, at some point they're bound to be right; all bull markets, sooner or later, turn into a bear market (though not necessarily with a resounding crash). However, if you're closely watching the indicators mentioned previously, you'll recognize it as a strong bull market, and instead of crashing, it keeps going higher. Even when the market has short pullbacks, it continues to rally.

Until there is evidence (which will be discussed in Chapter 5) that the bull market is coming to an end, it's a waste of energy and emotions to constantly fear a crash. It's also unusual for a market crash to occur in the middle of a bull market. On rare occasions, there is a "black swan" event—an unexpected and extreme news event that can cause a market crash and derail the bull market. Even then, the bull market will probably bounce back quickly.

Don't Fight the Tape

Not only should you not fight the Fed, but don't fight the stock market, either. There is an old Wall Street saying: "Don't fight the tape." This dates to the days when stock prices appeared on a ticker tape. Although technology has progressed, the saying is still valid. If the market trend is up, if the stock board is flashing green, then ride the market as long and as far as you can.

During bull markets, the market tends to ignore bad news—a clue that you are really in a bull market. Therefore, it is not advisable to fight it no matter how many problems there are in the economy or the world.

Some investors or traders, distrusting the power of the bull market, not only move to cash but may bet against the bull market by selling short—that is, they sell shares they don't currently own intending to purchase them later at a lower price. These doubters, rather than making money, all too often lose money. Why? Because they were wrong: If you are in the middle of a raging bull market, think of it as a freight train barreling down the tracks. Selling short stocks during a bull market is like stepping in front of the train, hoping it will stop before it hits you.

Remember the earlier comment: The market can go higher than you ever believed possible (conversely, as we'll see, it can also go lower than you ever thought possible). During a bull market, the market seems unstoppable.

Digging Deeper Into a Stock Chart

Now let's return to our discussion of charts and their importance in determining the state of the market. If you look at a long-term chart of the major market indexes (such as the S&P 500) during a bull market, you will see that the market (and many individual stocks) have made a series of higher highs and higher lows. In other words, the market keeps going higher, and after a pullback, it climbs higher than the previous high, or the previous low. This is confirmation of a continuing bull market.

Other technical indicators such as *moving averages* signal that the market is going higher. Basically, moving averages show the average value of a security's price over the duration of a specific period such as the last 50, 100, or 200 days. When moving averages are displayed on a chart, it's easy to see the current market trend. Traders also use moving averages to help make buying or selling decisions.

For example, during a bull market, if the major market indexes rise above their 200-day moving average, that is a significant buy signal. Even long-term buy-and-hold investors who use fundamental analysis pay attention to the 200-day moving average.

During a bull market, the price of the S&P 500 may rise above its 50-day, 100-day, and 200-day moving average. Moving averages are very popular with traders and investors because they help confirm the market's direction. At a glance, you can see where the market is headed—up or down.

Market Mastery

Pay attention to moving averages, especially the 50-day, 100-day, and 200-day MA.

In addition to moving averages, another reliable indicator is Moving Average Convergence/Divergence (MACD). This indicator consists of two lines: (1) a solid black line called MACD, and (2) a red line (sometimes dotted) called the 9-day signal line. The signal line is slower because technically it's a moving average of the MACD line (yes, it's a moving average of a moving average). During a bull market, MACD will be pointing up, crossing over the zero line and its 9-day signal line. When the MACD line, which is the faster of the two lines, crosses above or below the 9-day signal line, this is significant.

If you follow MACD's calm, long-term signals, it should lead you in the right direction (it's especially good at identifying market bottoms). Moving averages and MACD are easy to interpret and understand, and they will help you to stay on the right side of the trend. Both of these technical indicators can be found on any chart program.

Note, however, that although these indicators work well when the market is trending up or down, they are not as effective during a sideways market. Also, there is always the risk that the indicators will give false signals, which is why you should not rely solely on indicators to make your investment decisions.

Another sentiment indicator is the Chicago Board Options Exchange Market Volatility Index. That's a mouthful, so it's usually known as VIX, or the volatility index. It has been used to indicate whether investors are complacent or fearful. This is a contrarian indicator, meaning that when investors show no fear of the downside, the probability is that the market will reverse direction. Why? History has shown that investors are usually afraid (or greedy) at the wrong time. There's a popular saying about the VIX: When the VIX is high, it is time to buy, and when the VIX is low, it's time to go (sell). Although sentiment indicators such as VIX are useful for gauging the mood of the crowd, they are not as effective for timing. As mentioned earlier, sentiment readings can remain at extreme levels for a long time before the market reverses direction.

If you are unfamiliar with technical, fundamental, or sentiment indicators and want more detailed explanations, read my book *All About Market Indicators* (McGraw-Hill).

Everyone Is a Genius in a Bull Market

As the market reaches all-time highs (and this can take years), many investors and traders who have been making a lot of money during the bull market come to believe they are stock-picking geniuses. You may even hear stories about friends or acquaintances who have taken up day trading to reap high profits.

The higher the market goes, the more bullish Wall Street is; some financial experts may proclaim that this bull market is unstoppable. (At investment seminars, many money managers are wildly bullish during the later stages of a bull market.)

As the market climbs, more retail investors believe the market will never go down. Some go on margin, attempting to double down on their stock purchases. In fact, during the later stages of many bull markets, margin debt levels skyrocket. This means that greedy investors or traders are borrowing money to buy even more stocks and ETFs.

Conversely, short sellers and some bear market analysts get angry at this stage, warning that the bull market can't go any higher.

Don't be swayed by their visions of doom. As mentioned earlier, if you attempt to bet against a raging bull market, you may go broke (before you're eventually proven right).

The Parabolic Melt-up

Sometimes bull markets go up so fast and high that it shocks investors and traders. During the melt-up stage, most short sellers have given up, and many bearish columnists are so humiliated that they stop warning of a crash. (Actually, when too many short sellers go quiet, that is a signal the bull market may end sooner rather than later, but we'll get to that further on.)

When the market goes parabolic, if you are on the long side, you won't believe how much money you are making. By "parabolic," we mean that stock prices go straight up, defying market gravity. Investors are giddy, along with anyone who works on Wall Street. At this stage, you'll see panic buying as investors are afraid they are going to miss out on the rising stock prices.

As buyers rush in to buy anything that moves, stocks or indexes will zoom up in a straight line well above their 100-day and 200-day moving averages. Also, MACD will rise above and beyond its 9-day signal line. Although market indexes don't go parabolic very often, penny stocks often do, which is why penny stocks are so risky to trade. After all, what goes up must come down.

When the market (or a stock) goes parabolic, it reflects excessive buying enthusiasm. However, astute investors and traders know that a melt-up is a panic-inducing occurrence. Just as frightened investors *capitulate* (sell in a panic) as the market nears a bottom, a rapidly rising market induces investors to buy in a panic because they are afraid of missing out on a huge rally. Instead of celebrating a parabolic market, that rocketlike rise is a clue that the bull market's days may be ending. When it appears as if the stock market is giving away free money and everyone seems to be winning, that is a clue that you should consider moving to cash. The best approach as the rally continues is to scale out of the market and sell more of your holdings. However, do not sell everything until you get a confirmed bear signal.

The Climax

At the final stage of some bull markets, the market reaches a climax. It doesn't matter why, but it happens. If you're brave enough (or silly enough) to short the market at this price level, you could lose a fortune. Of course, you could be right about the market, and even recognize a market top. That is when you can short stocks, planning to cover at a lower price. If your market call is good and the market falls, you reap big bucks during a bear market. But if you time it wrong, the market will teach you a lesson that you'll never forget. Rather than betting against the market, most astute investors or traders sit quietly and wait for the market to stop climbing.

Market Mastery

Don't short a bull market that appears unstoppable. There will be many opportunities in the future to go short, if you have the patience to sit and wait.

Not every bull market goes parabolic because every market is different. However, when it appears to you that the market could be forming a bubble, you should be wary. At the moment, all you know is that investors and traders can't buy stocks fast enough. At this point, there is a buying frenzy.

The End of the Bull Market

Eventually, the bull market ends and the market slows down or reverses direction. It can come in one dramatic correction, in short selloffs, or even in wave after wave of selling. Wall Street and its followers are now in disbelief. They will tell you a dozen reasons why the market is going down—and here's the interesting part: They always tell you it's coming back quickly, and most investors believe them. After all, financial institutions as well as millions of individual investors are programmed to think the market always goes up.

In the next chapter, we'll discuss what to buy during a bull market, especially if you can identify it in the early stages.

CHAPTER 3

What to Buy in a Bull Market

When the market is bullish, especially in its early stages, it's a great time to be an investor or trader. After all, almost all bullish strategies are profitable (although it is still possible for undisciplined traders to lose money). In this chapter we'll discuss various types of securities you can buy during a bull market.

Greed and Fear

If you are reading this during a bull market, enjoy the ride, because it could last several years. Even though you must never stop analyzing the market and watching indicators, bull markets can be extremely profitable if you are patient. However, you must always be cautious and aware.

So what should you buy during a bull market? Everything! I'm kidding, but not entirely. When the stock market is bullish, almost all stocks rally, but not necessarily all asset classes. There are profits for nearly everyone who owns the right asset type.

We are often our own worst enemies, and many investors (including some pros) mishandle bull markets. After all, bull markets seem easy to trade because the market does all of the heavy lifting. Even in a bull market, however, you must balance the twin emotions of greed and fear, and that's not easy to do.

It's easy to be greedy during a bull market, especially during the later stages when stock prices are accelerating. That greed can cost money if you are unwilling to accept the possibility that the market will eventually reverse direction.

Conversely, if you are overly afraid of a correction or crash during a bull market, you may be underinvested and lose potential profits. On the one hand, you want to be invested during a bull market. On the other hand, you should protect your assets in case of a disaster.

What to Buy: Individual Stocks or Market Indexes?

No matter which strategy you use, one of your first decisions is whether to invest in individual stocks or indexes. In my opinion, during a bull market, most investors and traders should buy ETFs that track the major market indexes, or index mutual funds.

Here's why: Most people are terrible stock pickers. Often they get their stock picks from acquaintances, an article they read, or a know-it-all on a financial television program. Few investors take the time to study the fundamentals of a company, and that means analyzing balance sheets, determining the true value of a company, and having the discipline to hold that stock for the long term (years or decades). If you pick the wrong stock, you will lose money and perhaps spend years trying to get back to even.

Most people have neither the time nor patience to master the art of picking the right stocks. Therefore, I believe that investing in index funds or index ETFs is the best choice for novice investors. Yes, it's true that disciplined investors such as Warren Buffett and Peter Lynch (and several others) have shown that if you pick the right stocks at the right time and hold them for decades, you can make a fortune.

However, each year, more than 80 percent of professional mutual fund managers do not beat the market averages (a statistic that is confirmed annually). Disciplined wizards such as Buffett and Lynch are the exception, and few beginners (or the majority of pros) can emulate their success. It takes years to learn the required skills and develop the necessary discipline to be a successful investor or trader.

This isn't to discourage you entirely from buying individual stocks, because with the power of a bull market behind you it's possible you will do very well in the market. Nevertheless, if you're holding stocks, don't forget that it's easy to lose your gains, especially if you're not monitoring underlying conditions.

Another problem with buying individual stocks is that even stocks of great companies can decline by 10 percent or more during bull markets when those companies are hit with bad news. It takes an incredible amount of patience to hold a stock through these dips. You also have to do extensive research to separate the winning stocks from the losers, and that's not easy for most people.

Market Mastery

There's an easy way to compare owning an individual stock with owning an index mutual fund or index ETF. Let's say you own a high-quality, dividend-paying Dow stock, and it goes down 15 percent because of a bad earnings report. If you owned the stock, you lost 15 percent. But if you owned an index fund or ETF that tracked the Dow, the index might go down by 1 or 2 percent that day. That is the power of diversification, and another advantage of owning an index rather than owning an individual stock. Even the best stocks go down, and if you own it, you will feel the pain. (Of course, if the stock had rallied by that same 15 percent, your gain would be far less if you owned the ETF.)

Bottom Line

Whether you buy individual stocks or index ETFs, recognizing when a bull market begins or ends is necessary. As you know, a rising tide lifts all boats, so if you are investing in stocks, it's a lot more profitable doing so in a bull market (when the tide is rising).

Keeping It Simple

From all this flows the most important suggestion for your investments: Keep it simple!

In a bull market everyone should have a core account of either index ETFs or index mutual funds. Even if you are determined to buy and sell individual stocks, having an index fund or ETF provides diversification, lowers cost, and increases simplicity. Your goal is not to beat the indexes during a bull market, which most pros can't do, but to match the indexes.

It's also true that when holding individual stocks, you can double or triple your gains with the right stocks. One strategy, therefore, is to have your core account in the indexes and a smaller account for speculating with stocks.

Why Index Funds Make Sense

Index funds—either index ETFs or index mutual funds— are inexpensive, are easy to understand, and provide instant diversification. Because you are trying to match the market, not beat it, you want to eliminate excessive trading expenses, which you can accomplish with these funds.

Let's compare an index fund with an actively traded mutual fund.

1. Mutual funds with an active manager are designed to beat the indexes. In fact, that is why you pay a little bit more for mutual funds that are actively managed (sometimes a lot more, but it depends on the fund).

2. Many actively managed mutual funds are required to remain fully invested in stocks, even during a bear market. By the rules of some funds (look at the fund's prospectus for details), fund managers cannot sell their stocks and move everything to cash (they are limited to how much cash they can hold at any given time). Index funds do not have this problem because they make no effort to beat the market. Their objective is to match the performance of their benchmark index as closely as possible, which is why they are always fully invested.

Here's the benefit of owning an actively managed mutual fund: If you are in a mutual fund with an excellent fund manager, he or she may beat the market. For example, if the market falls by 15 percent in one year, a good fund manager may only lose 5 percent. (If you owned an index fund, you'd lose 15 percent that year.)

Conversely, if the market rose by 10 percent, a winning fund manager might make 15 percent, beating the market average. (If you owned an index fund, you'd have a 10 percent return that year.)

It's true that there are excellent fund managers who beat the market averages almost every year and may provide fantastic profits for their investors. If you find that rare mutual fund manager (or money manager) who can do both (offer profits and protection), then by all means let him manage your account. Keep in mind that how this manager did in the past is not a guarantee of how well he'll do in the future.

Now for the bad news: As mentioned earlier, less than 20 percent of mutual fund managers beat the indexes each year. In other words, if you buy and hold an index fund, you will beat more than 80 percent of the fund managers.

If you bought and held some actively managed mutual funds through a vicious bear market, the chances are good you'll have to wait several years (sometimes a decade) to get back to even.

Fortunately, the market has always come back, but if you choose the wrong mutual fund, your account might not.

It's your choice whether to pay extra for an actively managed mutual fund or money manager. If you do find an excellent no-load mutual fund (no-load means that no sales commission is charged), continue to monitor your investments. The biggest mistake you can make is to give anyone *carte blanche* over your account.

Bottom Line

Actively managed mutual funds work for many people, but expenses are higher than with an index fund. If you can find a superb mutual fund manager who consistently beats the indexes, those extra expenses might be worth it. If not, stick with an index fund.

Get Started with Indexing

To get started with index funds, you can buy either index ETFs or index mutual funds. Either provides instant diversification and lower costs than traditional mutual funds. ETFs are more convenient (they trade like stocks and are easy to buy and sell). Neither the index ETF nor the index mutual fund is actively managed.

The following are four of the most popular *nonleveraged* ETFs that mimic the performance of indexes:

1. SPY (the 500 stocks included in the S&P 500 index)
2. DIA (the 30 stocks included in the Dow Jones Industrial Average)
3. QQQ (the 100 stocks in the Nasdaq-100)
4. IWM (the 2,000 stocks in the Russell 2000)

If you want to diversify, you can buy ETFs that track gold (GLD), emerging markets (EEM), a bond ETF, or an ETF that includes stocks that pay dividends (VIG), to name a few. You can also keep some of your assets in cash. During a bull market, the bulk of your portfolio should be in stock index funds, but diversifying into other asset classes is appropriate for most investors.

Market Mastery

When this book discusses ETFs it mean ETFs that track the major market indexes. Although there are thousands of ETFs, and new products are created each day, stick with the broad-based indexes. The ones listed previously are the most popular, but there are many other ETF products.

Stay Away from Leveraged ETFs

Note that the four ETFs mentioned earlier are not leveraged—that is to say, they don't attempt to increase returns of the underlying index by borrowing money or including complex products such as futures contracts. Leveraged ETFs attempt to double or triple the daily return of the underlying index, while the ETFs recommended here stick with straight returns. For example, if you buy SPY (the index for the S&P 500), and the S&P 500 goes up by 1 percent, SPY will also go up by approximately 1 percent. That is a 1 to 1 correlation, which means that SPY is not leveraged.

If you buy a leveraged ETF, it is essentially the same as using margin. For a $1 investment, you own $2 worth of a stock portfolio. When the S&P 500 moves 1 percent in either direction, the ETF rises or falls by 2 percent. You can even buy ETFs with 3 to 1 leverage. How exciting!

Leveraged ETFs are designed for day traders. It is important *not* to purchase leveraged ETFs as long-term holdings. The arithmetic may not be obvious, but because leveraged ETFs are rebalanced every day, it results in extra trading and slippage expenses (losses due to buying near the ask price and selling near the bid price). That causes a slow erosion of the ETF's value over time.

Bottom Line

Although leveraged ETFs are a brilliant marketing idea (promising that you can double or triple your investment), it's best to avoid investing in them. The ETFs that make the most sense for our purposes have a 1 to 1 relationship with the index. If the index rises by 3 percent, so does the ETF.

Index Mutual Funds

Just like ETFs, index mutual funds do not have an active manager, which is why they have low expenses. A significant difference between ETFs and index mutual funds, however, is how they are bought and sold.

ETFs have bid and ask prices that change throughout the day, so you can buy and sell them like stocks. On the other hand, the net asset value (NAV) of index mutual funds are calculated only once, at the end of the day.

Almost all mutual fund families provide low-cost index funds that emulate the major indexes. In addition, if you are enrolled in a 401(k) (or IRA), you will likely have a choice of index funds.

The three largest no-load mutual fund families that have index funds are Fidelity, Vanguard, and T. Rowe Price, but there are many more fund families to choose from. It's your choice as to which family provides you the best performance and value.

Should you choose index ETFs or index mutual funds? It depends. If you buy and hold during a bull market and rarely trade, then either index funds or ETFs will meet your needs. If you have a trader's instinct, however, ETFs are more desirable because they are traded just like stocks. In addition, ETFs have no redemption fees, while mutual funds do.

If you are a client of a brokerage firm, you can choose index ETFs or index mutual funds. On the other hand, if you have a 401(k) plan at a company, your only choice is likely to be index mutual funds (although that depends on your company).

If you're not interested in having someone else manage your investments, you have another choice: You can buy individual stocks.

If You Decide to Buy Individual Stocks

Not everyone likes buying and selling indexes because they are not exciting. Also, if you pick the right stock, you can make many times your investment and handily beat the market averages. As you were previously warned, however, you can also lose money. Here's the main point: If even most of the professional mutual fund managers can't beat the market each year, what are the chances that we can? Still, if you believe you are a talented stock picker, then by all means start researching stocks to buy.

Most important: Even if you choose individual stocks, it is essential to be aware of overall market conditions. For example, taking a long position (i.e., going long) on a technology stock in a bear market might be a recipe for disaster. In a bull market, however, that same stock has a better chance of turning into a wise investment. Why? As I said before, a rising tide lifts all boats.

The Pros and Cons of Individual Stocks

The allure of stocks is that you can make a lot of money, and quickly. Super stock pickers such as Buffett and Lynch have proven that it is possible. If you choose the right stocks and make money, you can also receive dividends (assuming the company pays dividends).

Unfortunately, many people lose fortunes in stocks. As mentioned earlier, most people are terrible stock pickers, and in reality, few people can predict which stocks will do well over the long term, even based on the fundamentals.

Yet, if you're able to create a diversified portfolio of individual stocks (at least ten), and adjust the percentages of each stock to a level that matches your risk tolerance, goals, and time frame, then you can manage your own stock portfolio. Alternatively, you can hire someone else to do it for you or invest in a mutual fund. That's exactly what most people do, because they do not feel qualified to make their own investment decisions. In bull markets, it works out well, as most trades become profitable.

Problems arise, of course, when a bear market appears. Few people manage to get out of their holdings in time without taking a huge hit. Others try to hold their stocks through the bear market, though they must have nerves of steel. We'll discuss all of this in the forthcoming chapter on bear markets.

This isn't to discourage you completely from buying individual stocks, but you need to know the truth. Buying and selling individual stocks is not an easy route to earning big money. When the market turns against you, it can be downright treacherous. At least with the indexes you have a fighting chance.

Even in a moderate bull market or sideways market, many stocks are one bad earnings report away from a selloff. It's worse with penny stocks (avoid buying them) and even many small-cap stocks. If you must buy individual stocks, buy well-known, liquid stocks that pay dividends.

On a more positive note, sometimes a unique buying opportunity comes along, such as a company you discovered in its early stages. If you can find a business such as Home Depot, Lowe's, McDonald's, Google, Apple, or Starbucks when it is starting out, you can make a fortune buying and holding stocks. Easy? No. Possible? Yes. Finding relatively inexpensive stocks that are about to take off is the goal of most long-term investors.

Trade Stocks or Indexes?

What should you buy in a bull market? Buy the indexes, as either an ETF or an index mutual fund. Nevertheless, you must buy and sell what makes sense for you and brings you the most profits. Start with a simple strategy such as buying and selling the indexes before trading or investing in individual stocks.

It can't be stressed enough that buying indexes is a simpler and less costly method of participating in the market. Wait until you gain more experience before picking and choosing stocks (if you ever do).

Of course, buying the indexes is not a wildly popular choice. After all, financial professionals depend on you, the retail investor, to buy and sell stocks. But it's funny: When you stop thinking of individual stocks, your mind is clear of the annoying tips, news, and hype. If you turn on one of the many financial shows, at times you may feel as if you're at a casino. "Buy this stock! Buy that stock! Hit it big! Get rich!" The indexes may not be as exciting, but you will probably sleep better at night. You no longer have to listen to people touting the latest hot stock, or read mindless articles on the top ten stocks to buy. You don't need to believe friends or acquaintances with a "can't lose" stock tip.

Bottom Line

Whatever you choose to buy, make sure you buy during a bull market. When the market is on your side, it's amazing how quickly you can build wealth.

Now that we have ideas of what to buy in a bull market, in the next chapter we will look at some of the strategies you can use.

CHAPTER 4

Bull Market Strategies

In this important chapter we'll discuss a few of the most useful strategies you should follow in a time of market growth, as well as a few to avoid. The goal of these strategies is to keep things simple for you. The more complicated the strategy, the greater the risk. Although many investors believe that a sexy-sounding strategy is needed to make money, this is not true.

How to Trade in a Bull Market

Trading in a bull market is enjoyable because most equity strategies work, from buy-and-hold to short-term trading. After all, most stocks follow the uptrend. Holding during a bull market is relatively easy because everyone believes that profits will continue to grow.

Some cautious bulls may move some of their investment dollars to cash for safety, and that's wise. It's always acceptable to take some money off the table. Nevertheless, it is also suggested that you stay the course until you see clues (more on finding them later) that convince you to take defensive action. It feels good to exit before any decline begins, but bull (or bear) markets can last much longer than anticipated. You don't want to leave money on the table, and you don't want to miss out completely on the final bull market surge, if there is one.

As the market climbs, some financial writers, and perhaps some of your acquaintances, will be suspicious of the market's ability to rise further. They may predict that the market can't go any higher and is topping out. Many people don't realize, or forget, that the market can go much higher, especially when a majority of investors are in disbelief. Also, it's easy to get scared out of a bull market because others are so skittish. That's why it's so important to find your own clues and follow any signals.

Don't forget that the market moves higher (or lower) based on human emotion as much as on reality. It's also based on the perceptions of what institutional investors are doing. There could be terrible economic news, world turmoil, and lousy corporate earnings, but the market can still go up.

It's essential to realistically assess overall market conditions. It's true that during a bull market, there will be pullbacks, and even an occasional correction. As long as the overall trend is up, however, it is still a bull market, and you do not want to have all your holdings in cash. In a bull market, investors tend to ignore negative news. This may not make sense, it may not be realistic . . . but that is the way it is.

Sell your holdings only when you have a good reason to do so. Just because you "think" the rally will end is not a good enough reason. Base decisions on your charts and actual evidence, not on emotion. It's good to take some cash off the table when you are uncomfortable, but do not sell all of your ETFs, funds, or stocks because of fear. Also, don't sell in a panic because you read a negative article, or an acquaintance warns you of an imminent stock market crash. Review evidence, observations, and indicators before doing anything drastic to your portfolio.

At the same time, you should monitor the market regularly (once a week is often enough for most people). If you recognize clues that the bull market is faltering—it could take years for this to happen—then you will want to take steps to protect your profits.

There is nothing worse for your ego and account balance than to watch a winning position turn into a losing one.

Holding through a temporary pullback is fine. You can't try to catch every market move (unless you're a short-term trader), but you want to be out of the market before the next bear market appears. Fortunately, you usually have enough time to get out, unless there is a black swan event, which cannot be predicted.

In fact, knowing when to take profits is one of the most difficult decisions you have to make. If the market keeps going higher, then the odds are good that the bull market will continue.

On the other hand, if investors are overly bullish (i.e., irrationally exuberant), that is a signal that the market may be getting too frothy—that is, the market rises above its true value based on little substance but high demand. But keep this in mind: Judging by past booms (and busts), the excessive bullishness and overbought conditions can last longer than anyone thinks is possible. There are also precautions you can take to protect some of your assets, which I'll discuss in Chapter 12. (These include buying put options, hedging, and moving to cash.)

Bottom Line

In a bull market, it's easy to buy. The hard part is making and keeping profits before the next bear market appears.

With all this in mind, here are the key strategies you should consider in a bull market.

Strategy #1: Buy and Hold Stocks (but Not Forever)

The buy-and-hold strategy has been drilled into the minds of investors for decades. The idea is to buy stock in a fundamentally sound company and hold it for the long term (think in term of years). As long as it remains a sound investment and you have no reason to sell, you'll receive a satisfactory return on your investment.

The beauty of buy-and-hold is that you can buy a stock and watch it rise in price without doing anything. Buy-and-hold is the easiest investment strategy to use. During bull markets it works wonderfully.

The problem with buy-and-hold is that most people don't have the skills to find the right stocks, nor do they have the patience to hold for decades without selling. They also don't have the discipline, after buying a losing stock, to sell or admit they made a mistake.

In addition, when the market changes from bull to bear, buy-and-hold becomes a difficult path to follow as the value of your holdings steadily declines. Typically, as the bear market continues, too many investors finally decide that they can't take any more pain, and sell all their stocks just as the bear market cycle is ending.

Many people who buy and hold don't realize that they must occasionally reevaluate and rebalance their holdings. The strategy is not buy and forget. Buy-and-hold works during bull markets, but it's not a guaranteed investment method.

Here's a suggestion for investors: Rather than buying and holding forever, buy and hold stocks until something fundamentally or technically changes in the company. This is how buy-and-hold should work, but it requires more effort on your part. One of the reasons that indexes make sense is that you don't have to pick winning and losing stocks. After all, it's extremely difficult for even the pros to find the right company to buy and hold.

Strategy #2: Buy and Hold Index ETFs (but Not Forever)

Buying and holding ETFs that match indexes makes more sense than buying individual stocks, as long as you don't buy and hold forever. As previously mentioned, long-term investors and long-term traders should buy and hold until the trend changes or there are clues a bear market is approaching.

The biggest mistake that buy-and-holders make is blindly following this strategy without reacting when market conditions change. If the market pulls back, falling below certain technical levels (which you'll read about later), that is a sell signal, and it is time to reduce your positions. If the market keeps falling, you will reduce even more or get out completely.

Legendary investors such as Warren Buffett and Peter Lynch will hold individual stocks during bear markets, but then again they have teams of analysts working for them who can determine the fair value of any stock. Also, the creator of the first index fund, John Bogle, buys and holds index funds during every market. He believes it is next to impossible for retail investors to know when to get in and when to get out.

It's hard to argue with the success of these super investors, who are patient, disciplined, and focused. If you have a long time frame and have the personality traits of the best buy-and-holders, then you can stay the course through the next bear market by not selling.

After all, through the entire history of the stock market, the market has always come back, even though it can take years. The real questions are: How long will it take to recover from the next bear market, and will you need your invested assets before then? On the other hand, if you have technical or fundamental evidence (opinions don't count) that a bull market is coming to an end or is struggling, there's nothing wrong with reducing your long positions and even getting out completely.

Most people say that it's impossible to time the market. It's true that no one can time the exact top or the exact bottom, but you can buy early enough to take advantage of the next bull market and get out early enough to prevent losses from the next bear market.

Bottom Line

By all means buy and hold, but not permanently, and only until the current (bullish) trend ends. We'll discuss buy-and-hold during a bear market in a later chapter.

Strategy #3: Dollar Cost Averaging

Dollar cost averaging is an old but popular investment strategy. If you are buying and holding mutual funds, index funds, or index ETFs, dollar cost averaging can be profitable. It's even better if you are using this strategy as part of a company 401(k) plan or IRA.

When you dollar cost average, you invest a set amount of money (e.g., $250) for a set period (e.g., every two weeks). If using this strategy in a company plan such as a 401(k), you can ask your employer to deduct that amount from your paycheck.

The idea behind dollar cost averaging is to buy more shares at a lower price at regular intervals. Basically, you buy more shares when prices are low and buy fewer shares when prices are high. By investing a fixed amount on a set time schedule, you don't have to try to time the market.

It should be stressed that this strategy primarily works during a bull market. If you follow it during a bear market, you are adding to a losing portfolio with little hope of a positive return, that is, until the bear market ends.

This strategy is primarily suited for buy-and-hold investors. In addition, the strategy works well with index funds or index ETFs rather than individual stocks. Why? If you choose the wrong stock, you will be dollar cost averaging right into the ground.

Strategy #4: Buy High and Sell Higher

Although buying high and selling higher appears to defy logic and common sense, it works as long as you use strict money management tactics (discussed in Chapter 12). This strategy, first introduced by Jesse Livermore, is to buy stocks that have reached all-time highs. The theory behind the strategy is that strong stocks keep going higher, while weaker stocks go lower. (William O'Neil expanded on this stock approach by creating additional buy-and-sell rules using CAN SLIM, his stock picking strategy. By the way, if you decide to buy and sell individual stocks, using a system like CAN SLIM is recommended.)

In a strong bull market, buy high and sell higher often works brilliantly as leading stocks continue to climb. Those who believe the market "can't go any higher" are shocked when it does. (On the other hand, if the market weakens or changes directions, you must use strict money management tactics such as stop losses—an order that instructs the broker to enter an order to sell (or buy) when the price falls (or rises) to a designated level—to avoid losing money.)

Buying the major market indexes while they are on the way up can be a winning plan. As long as you monitor positions closely and begin selling when you detect a trend change, this is a very effective strategy. If anything, you are adding to winning positions.

Like any other strategy, there is risk. At some point, bull markets end and stocks stop moving higher. If you're trading stocks, it's essential that you sell when they begin to pull back. Although you must choose your own price level trigger, a 5 to 7 percent pullback would be significant.

You also don't want to trade in every market environment. One of the advantages of investing in an index is that they are usually less volatile than individual stocks. If you are buying and selling individual stocks, you must monitor positions very closely.

Conversely, trading a diversified index fund offers less risk, and requires less attention.

Strategy #5: Buy on the Dip

This strategy is the opposite of buy high and sell higher. The idea is that when a stock or index falls in price, you buy more shares. Although this strategy does work when the pullback is temporary, it's risky.

The theory behind buy on the dip is that in a bull market your stock, even after experiencing a loss, will bounce back. Use this strategy when the stock has strong fundamentals (earnings growth, revenue growth, etc.), and has not given a significant sell signal (such as breaking through *support*), which you'll read about shortly.

In theory, buy on the dip feels as if you are getting a bargain. Instead of dollar cost averaging, where you buy a specified amount for a specified time period, with buy on the dip you buy whenever the stock price is appealing.

In reality this is a risky strategy, as once many stocks start to fall they keep falling. I've seen some of the best and most popular stocks fall from their all-time highs, and as the stock falls, buy-on-the-dippers step in to accumulate more shares. Unfortunately, there aren't enough buyers to prop up the stock and it keeps falling.

For example, stocks in excellent companies such as Citigroup (NYSE:C) and other financial stocks were at all-time highs in 2007 when they started to plunge. Numerous institutions and individual investors owned Citi, and as it fell, investors stepped in to buy more shares.

Citi eventually leveled off at $3 per share before making a comeback during the next bull market. Anyone who bought this stock on the dip lost a lot of money.

Bottom Line

If you are going to adopt this risky strategy, be sure you're in a bull market and that the stock is still technically sound. Don't forget that any stock (no matter how popular or how high) or index can fall to price levels from which it's impossible to recover.

Market Mastery

With certain stocks that remain within a range, buy on the dip is an effective strategy. For example, if a stock you are following stays within a range of $50 and $60, you simply buy as it falls near $50 and sell when it approaches $60. As long as the stock stays within that range, you can make money.

Nevertheless, you must use strict money management rules. In this example, if you buy the stock at $50 on the dip and it keeps falling, you must sell immediately.

I've made some references to support and resistance. Because these concepts are so important in technical analysis, I am giving them a quick review. If you're an experienced stock trader, feel free to skip this section.

Support and Resistance

Here's how *support* works: When a stock is falling, it will pass through certain prices on the way down at which enough buyers purchase the shares to "support" the price and prevent it from falling further. *Support* is the price level at which a stock price found support the last time it traded down to this level. In theory, the same price will provide support again because buyers have confidence that the price level will hold. However, if buyers fail to appear, or if they are overwhelmed by sellers, then that support price will be broken. That is a significant sell signal.

Conversely, when a stock price is rising, there will be certain prices on the way up at which sellers step in and may prevent the stock from rising further. *Resistance* refers to the price level at which a stock has stopped rising previously and sellers step into the market and take temporary control. When the stock is not expected to go any higher, traders sell their shares (or sell short), which halts upward momentum. There isn't enough demand for the stock to cause it to rise any higher.

How do sellers "prevent" the stock from moving higher? They can't. However, those who believe the stock will move through resistance continue to hold. If a sufficient number of buyers enters the marketplace, or when the sellers give up, upward pressure on the stock returns and resistance is broken. Buyers are once again in charge. Technical analysts consider the breaking of resistance to be a significant buy signal. It also brings new buyers into the market, often driving prices higher. Note: Many technicians use moving averages as support and resistance.

Strategy #6: Buy Low and Sell High

Similar to buy on the dip, the "buy low and sell high" mantra has been drilled into investors since the early days of the stock market. Unfortunately, this cliché has caused many investors to lose big in the market, and here's why. First, the terms "low" and "high" are difficult to define. Although telling someone to "buy low" sounds reasonable, what does "low" really mean? It could be a low P/E ratio or the stock's fifty-two-week low. In reality, it's not wise to buy low when prices are declining rapidly.

Also, what is "high"? Do you sell when a stock nears its fifty-two-week high, or do you wait and hope that your stock price will break out to a new high? The fact is that no one knows what is low or what is high until after stocks have already reached those points.

Bottom Line

Buying low and selling high sounds brilliant, but in the real world, it's difficult to accomplish, especially if you are trying to find "the" low or "the" high. Your goal is to try to buy at a relatively low price and sell at a higher price. Buy when the market is in an uptrend, and sell or reduce your positions when the market becomes dangerous, or is in a downtrend.

Market Mastery

In the heat of battle, after a stock has fallen, it's impossible to know if the current price is a good entry point. Thus, it's more important to focus on the market's signals rather than picking a bottom (or top). Those who missed an opportunity to buy will often complain, "If only I had bought XYZ! I would have made a fortune." They forget that at the time, buying XYZ for $20 per share was a risk. It could have fallen to $10 or less. So the next time you get mad at yourself for not buying at the low, don't forget that buying low (and selling high) is not realistic.

Bernard Baruch, a successful financier and economist, said of this strategy: "Don't try to buy at the bottom or sell at the top. It can't be done, except by liars."

Strategy #7: Speculating with Call Options

If you're a short-term trader, you can buy call options for speculation. This requires a little explanation. There are only two types of options: *calls* and *puts*. And with these two types of options, you can take only two actions: buy or sell. Although there are dozens of fancy sounding options strategies, every strategy is based on buying or selling calls or puts. Owning a call option is similar to "going long" a stock. If you believe that the option's underlying stock will go up in price, you could buy a call. When the underlying stock does go up in price, the call option usually follows. The attractive part about owning call options is that you can participate in the upswing of a stock without actually owning the stock—and for a lot less money.

Keep in mind that most speculators lose money when trading options, primarily because they do not understand how options work. To make money when buying calls, you must not only know whether the stock is moving higher, but you must also be an excellent market timer. Nevertheless, because of leverage (a small investment controlling many more dollars' worth of stock), it is tempting to buy call options because you can make many times your investment during bull markets. Although further discussion of options is outside the scope of this book, to learn more about this fascinating subject, I suggest reading my book *Understanding Options* (McGraw-Hill, 2nd edition).

Strategy #8: Pyramiding (i.e., Scaling In or Out)

This strategy, first introduced by Jesse Livermore, is used by a number of top traders. Instead of committing all his investment dollars at one time, Livermore would pyramid (or scale) into a position; that is, he would buy only a limited number of shares at a time. If the stock performed as he expected, he'd buy more shares. If the stock didn't perform as he expected, he'd sell. Livermore also often used this strategy to test whether he was trading in a bull or bear market.

Let's say it's a bull market and you want to invest $3,000 in QQQ, the ETF for Nasdaq-100. Instead of buying $3,000 worth of shares at once, you scale into the position $1,000 at a time (some investors might scale in by purchasing a particular number of shares). If the purchase is profitable, you'll add to the position and spend another $1,000. By pyramiding into an ETF, you add to your position on the way up (see "Buy High and Sell Higher" strategy).

On the other hand, if QQQ goes down, you wait. If QQQ continues to fall, you sell the position and cut your losses. This was obviously not the correct time to buy. Instead of risking the entire $3,000, though, you only risked a third of it.

The downside to the strategy is that you pay extra commissions on multiple purchases, but because commissions are so low (often less than $10), this shouldn't concern you, although that depends on the size of your portfolio. Note: If you are starting out and are investing less than $1,000, it makes sense to buy all the shares at once.

Bottom Line

Every successful trade begins with your ability to assess current market conditions. If you cannot determine when we're in a bull, bear, or sideways market, then the methods described earlier may be too risky. Always know the market environment before using any of these strategies.

Strategy #9: Follow the Money

Although the market reflects the hopes and fears and greed of millions of investors and traders, institutional traders have the power to move stocks because they trade so many shares at one time, and that in turn moves the market. A substantial amount of trading volume is attributed to institutions (mutual funds, pension funds, banks, and hedge funds).

Therefore, if you want to make money in the market, it makes sense to "follow the money"—that is, to buy what the institutions are buying. Actually, institutional activity is reflected in the charts, indicators, and clues. So when you obey market signals, you are following the institutions.

An even better way to determine where major institutions are putting their money is by following trading volume (trading volume can be found at the bottom of a chart or on financial websites such as Google Finance and Yahoo! Finance).

You may ask, what moves large institutions to buy or sell? The answer: They are always receiving new money that has to be invested into the market. Because these institutions are constantly buying, that is another reason why the market always has an upside bias.

In fact, if you talk to most investors, they will probably argue that the market is going up (or is about to). Also, since the year-end bonuses of those who work on Wall Street (as well as their jobs) depend on a rising market, they almost always have a bullish view.

In any given year you should assume that the stock market will go up more often than it will move down. Of course it doesn't always happen that way, but everyone connected to the stock market wants the market to go up, and that's a very powerful force.

If the market declines, financial analysts suggest that you buy because stock prices are so low. Conversely, if the market goes up, they suggest you buy because you will miss out on the next move up. In other words, according to the pros, you always buy, and never sell.

Market Mastery

Institutions have the power to move individual stocks, and that in turn moves the market. That is why it's so important to study volume. For example, high volume means that institutions are participating in the market. In addition, be aware that institutions receive market-moving news faster than retail investors. Often the market will make a violent move up or down seconds before you have time to react. The rallies or selloffs that suddenly appear out of nowhere are important clues. Step aside and use the charts and indicators before you consider taking any action based on these sudden price changes.

In Summary

- During a bull market, buying and holding index funds or ETFs that track the major market indexes is an excellent strategy. Although there are no guarantees this will continue in the future, the market goes up more than it goes down. Betting your money on the U.S. stock market has always been a profitable decision, and judging by what has happened in the past, it is usually a winning strategy.
- Although it's hard to do, your best strategy in a bull market is to stay the course as the market goes higher, and not get scared out of your profitable position because of a pullback, world turmoil, or rumors. It's easy to lose faith in the stock market and your position because of unfounded fears. But if you rely on observations, charts, and indicators, and not opinion, you will have a better idea of whether to buy, hold, or sell.

In summary, it's important to monitor the underlying market, and buy and hold index funds or index ETFs during a bull market while looking for signs it may come to an end.

Unfortunately, bull markets do not go on forever, which leads us to the next chapter. In it, you will learn how to find clues that a bull market is coming to an end.

CHAPTER 5

When a Bull Market Ends

If you are reading this during a bull market, you must be on the lookout for clues that a bull market is coming to an end. This outcome is inevitable, since no market goes up forever. The clues are not always easy to detect, but over time you can learn to be an astute market observer and see them before others do.

Many investors, after being spoiled by a lengthy bull market, start to believe that the good times will continue indefinitely. It's human nature. If the market goes too high (or even becomes a bubble, which is a rare event), investors begin to believe that the market will never go down. Someone may proclaim that the bull market "is different this time." (Note that when investors believe that investing is risk-free, that is a red flag to you, and you should exercise caution in your investment strategy.)

Nevertheless, when a bull market comes to an end, although diversification may help soften the blow, it won't remove risk entirely. When your sell signals are triggered, especially if you own an all-stock or index portfolio, it is time to get out of the market.

It should be stressed here again that if you go through life worrying about the next stock market crash or correction, it's likely you will miss out on many profitable opportunities. However, when conditions suggest that a severe decline is likely, you must act.

Market Mastery

Each person has a different definition of acceptable risk. The amount of risk you can tolerate is probably different from your neighbor's. Therefore, any suggestions about setting limits must be adjusted to suit your financial comfort zone.

Nothing Lasts Forever

A bull market can end with a big bang or with a whimper—a death by a thousand pullbacks. A bull market that slowly runs out of steam is easier to predict, and the warning signs are more obvious. Nevertheless, those who don't want the party to end refuse to believe that their beloved bull market could be over. It's interesting to watch: At the beginning of a bull market, few investors believed it had started. At the end of a bull market, few accept that it's ending.

Even when there are clear signs that the market is struggling, many investors refuse to listen. After all, for years they heard all of the warnings and predictions, and none came true. So why should they pay attention now?

It's not fair to blame these people. After years of a continuous bull market (and remember that each bull market is different), numerous crash warnings begin to sound like the boy who cried wolf.

When a Bull Market Ends with a Whimper

No market goes straight up or down. When a bull market struggles, it will still have some good days as the bulls struggle to continue their ride upward. As a result, even some of the brightest financial professionals will argue that the bull market is taking a rest and is not in any danger. Some pros may claim that the market is due for another expansion. It's hard for people to change their attitude and accept that they might be wrong.

Even more annoying, on extreme days when the market falls sharply, the bearish columnists who have been wrong for years once again warn that there is going to be an imminent and massive crash. These scary warnings and predictions only confuse investors. Meanwhile, those on Wall Street are telling their clients to stay calm. After all, "The market always comes back," they insist.

Of course, many professional investors (as well as retail investors) solve the dual dilemma of wanting to get rich and not wanting to lose money by diversifying into bonds or cash equivalents. Thus, if their stock portfolio declines, the bond or cash portion of the portfolio reduces the pain. Diversification is an important strategy and is one of the reasons it's best to invest in indexes rather than individual stocks, since indexes are, by their nature, diverse.

Red Flags and Other Clues

Since every market is different, the clues that indicate the bulls are retreating may be hard to recognize, particularly if the turnaround is a gradual one. At first, the clues don't seem important. For example, there might be a sharp rise in the price of oil, a negative finding from an obscure economic report, or a spike in interest rates. At the time, this information seems insignificant, but these are actually warning signs, if you can recognize their importance.

Most bull markets last between one and seven years, but there are always exceptions. You must always be alert for fundamental and technical clues that a trend change is occurring. Focus on facts rather than opinion.

Price levels do not determine whether a bull market is about to end. Therefore, just because the stock market is at an all-time high doesn't mean it cannot go higher (at first).

Here are some of the clues to look for when a bull market is slowly coming to an end. (Caution: Instead of the end of a bull market, it's also possible that what you're seeing is a short-term correction. Therefore, don't take any of these clues individually as definitive sell signals; rather, look at the overall trend.)

1. Financial Writers and Retail Investors Are Extremely Bullish

This seems contradictory, but it's not. If the American Association of Individual Investors (AAII) and Investors Intelligence sentiment readings are higher than 65 or 70 percent, that is a clue that bullishness has reached extreme levels. Although the excessive levels of bullishness can continue for a long time, this is a red flag. Before some of the biggest crashes in history, investor sentiment was off the charts (over 70 percent). In fact, these two sentiment indicators have been uncannily predictive of downturns in the past. (As mentioned earlier, the survey results of AAII and Investors Intelligence Advisor Sentiment Survey can be found on my blog, *www.michaelsincere.com.*)

Just because you get a high sentiment reading doesn't mean you should run out and sell all your stocks or index funds, but it does mean that the crowd is too bullish, which is not a good sign. When investors start to get excessively greedy, that's when to look for an exit.

2. Retail Investors Are Buying Everything That Moves, and on Margin

If you notice that retail investors are pouring money into equity mutual funds and are even borrowing money to buy stocks, that is another red flag. Retail investors have a reliable record of gorging on stocks when the bull market is near its end. If too many investors are also buying on margin (borrowing from the brokerage to fund purchases), it shouldn't be long before a pullback occurs, and perhaps a correction or a long-term downturn.

3. It Seems Like Everyone Is in the Market with Loads of Stock Tips

In 1929, Joseph Kennedy (father of the future president) reportedly received a stock tip from the guy who shined his shoes. According to the story, Kennedy sold all of his stocks within a week. He knew—or guessed—that when everyone in the country is buying, it's time to sell.

I personally experienced this when I attended a bidding war on new townhome construction in South Florida in 2007. Hundreds of people lined up for hours, all holding $20,000 checks (in addition to the half dozen people that stood in line all night so they could be first). Every fifteen minutes, the builder announced that the price of the homes just went up. In other words, houses were being bid on like stocks, with buyers paying the ever-increasing asking prices. I learned that most of the people in line had no intention of living in the homes, but planned to sell (i.e., "flip") them as soon as possible.

I knew that this was not going to end well, and it didn't. When the townhomes were built a year later, the prices had crashed. New buyers disappeared, leaving the sellers holding unprofitable investments.

Often, the media gives clues that the market is becoming overbought. It reports stories about people getting rich by buying stocks, gold . . . whatever the flavor of the day is. Once the media reports it, that's usually a negative signal.

Market Mastery

The previous examples are circumstantial evidence that the stock market might be overheated. Often, investors can remain irrationally exuberant for a long time. By the time the last investor finds out that the stock market is giving away free money, it may be too late to get out without severe losses.

4. Negative Earnings Start to Matter

During the height of a bull market, investors ignore almost all bad news, including negative earnings reports. Certain stocks might get punished for a day, if at all. However, as the market falters, earnings, which were previously ignored by investors, suddenly matter.

In fact, as the market starts to turn over, investors begin to notice all the negative information that has been reported for months (or years). No one can predict when fundamental data stop being ignored, but this is another sign that the bull market may reverse direction.

After the market undergoes a decline, some companies suddenly announce they are having a bad quarter. It's like a dam that suddenly breaks, and all the bad news floods across Wall Street.

5. Failed Rallies

One important clue that a bull market is running out of steam is that the market fails to make new highs, and loses strength. From a technical standpoint, that is a very significant signal. If sellers start to overwhelm buyers, rallies will continue to fail, and there will be a selloff. If there are enough selloffs, the bull market could be on its last legs.

A chart showing a series of lower lows and lower highs is significant. This means there aren't enough new buyers entering to move the market higher. This scenario can play out over weeks or months, so it takes patience to benefit from it.

6. Irrational Hubris Dominates the Market

When the market gets to extreme levels, you will see signs of hubris (i.e., overconfidence) in investors. Every decade manifests foolishness in its own way, because as technology changes, those who have the most money (and those who pretend they do) flaunt it. Such overconfidence is often a sign that the bull market is coming to an end, and if the overspending gets worse, then the market may move into bubble territory.

In 1929, everyone was buying new electronic appliances on credit (credit was a new idea back then). Meanwhile, the rich bought new cars, yachts, and mink coats. In the early twenty-first century, one sign of the hubris was the super rich asking each other, "What's your tail number?" (After all, if you don't have your own private jet, you're not really rich.) Because human behavior never changes, before the end of every bull market, there are always signs of excess.

7. Unusual Market Behavior Becomes the Norm

There are times when different assets such as stocks, bonds, and commodities act in unusual ways. For example, the bond market might suddenly get crushed when the yields on the 10-year Treasury spike. Gold, instead of rallying, could also decline, and stocks, which usually sell off when interest rates rise, could rally instead. The point is, when you start to detect unusual behavior among the various asset classes, it's a clue that something strange may be brewing. Make a point of observing the indexes, as well as what is happening overseas. Like a detective, you have to put all the clues together, and if something doesn't feel right, don't ignore it. You may have to take action.

End-of-Day Selloffs

In addition to the clues mentioned previously, one indication that a bull market may be in trouble is when there are end-of-day selloffs. In particular, if the market starts off higher in the morning but sells off through the day (especially at the end of the day), that is a negative sign.

If the selloff is accompanied by high volume (which suggests that large institutions are selling), you should consider getting out. At the very least, it's a warning. It doesn't necessarily mean that the bull market is ending, but the probability of a short-term selloff is high. In addition, it's significant if the market attempts to rally during the day and fails. A selloff during the last hour may also mean that traders are afraid to hold overnight, perhaps because they fear geopolitical events or what could happen in the foreign markets.

If there is a failed rally, it means that there aren't enough buyers to propel the market higher. There's no need for immediate action on your part, but if the market cannot rise any higher, in addition to not rising above resistance, that is an indication of a potential selloff. It would be nice if there were a hard-and-fast rule, but there isn't. A failed rally *may* be significant: If the market continuously fails to go higher, a selloff could be near.

On the one hand, there are days when the market is selling off hard and Fed officials or other powerful individuals say something positive about the market and the market immediately reverses direction. On the other hand, when the market is selling off and ignores the soothing words of Fed officials or other influential investors, this may be an exit signal: The selloff is stronger and more significant than anyone realizes.

There's also this caveat: The market often gives false signals (especially technical signals), so you need to confirm with other indicators and clues before selling.

By now, you probably realize that knowing when to get out of the market is more of an art than a science. All of the clues listed earlier are red flags, and the more red flags, the more cautious you must be.

Market Mastery
It doesn't matter why the market is selling off, because you won't know that until later. All you need to know is that the market is sinking, and that is a warning sign.

Watch Volume

Make a point of monitoring daily market volume so that you know when it is high or low. If a rally occurs with high volume (especially if the market rises above resistance), that is a significant buy signal. Conversely, a selloff on high volume is a red flag (especially if the market falls below support). On days when there is a rally or selloff with high volume, you can feel the strength and power of the market as the institutions power the market higher or lower.

If the market rallies on low volume, this is usually a negative sign (but is not a sell signal). More than likely, the market will not have enough strength to continue going much higher, but that depends on which stocks are leading the way (either higher or lower).

For example, if speculative stocks are leading the way higher, that is a reason to be cautious and possibly scaling back on how much money you have invested in the market (it is a personal decision). Note: In the past, speculative stocks included highflyers such as Tesla Motors or Priceline, but the names change with every market.

To repeat, those red flags do *not* mean the bull market has ended. The market may be consolidating (resting) temporarily before pushing higher. But volume is an important indicator that you should monitor regularly.

Not just volume, but that elusive characteristic, momentum, also determines whether the selloff or rally is significant. In other words, if there is panic buying or panic selling, watch not only whether volume is high, but also the rate at which stock prices are accelerating (i.e., momentum). High momentum is an important clue that the market is overreacting. You do not want to get caught in the euphoria that is driving an overheated market. Eventually, that euphoria can turn to fear.

Your goal, of course, is to be out of the market before downward momentum reaches excessive levels, and to be in the market before upward momentum becomes too extreme. You can't always be in the right place at the right time, but you can try.

Although there are sophisticated technical indicators that measure momentum, for our purposes downward momentum is seen on days when the market is falling quickly on higher volume. The combination of higher volume and strong downward price action can take the market to extreme levels. (During bull markets, there is higher volume and strong upward momentum.)

Market Mastery

Some people get frustrated with technical analysis (and also fundamental analysis) because they want clear-cut signals when to buy and sell. Once again, technical analysis is an art, not a science. You must collect data and make decisions based on the best evidence that you can acquire. When you invest in the stock market, there are no absolutes. It is often not logical (invest in Treasuries if you want logic), and it's not always fair.

Bull Market Reversals and Head Fakes

Another significant signal that a downturn may be in the offing is intraday reversals on larger than normal volume. For example, if the market is moving higher during the day and suddenly reverses direction for no apparent reason (you'll probably find out the reason later), this is a bearish signal. It is not a mandatory sell signal, but it's another red flag, to be considered in the context of the other indicators mentioned earlier. If all, or most, of these red flags appear, you should get out of the market or scale out of the market until the warning signs have disappeared.

Conversely, if the market is falling and then reverses direction on higher than normal volume, this is a bullish signal. Those who were shorting the market often cover their positions, and that buy-side volume drives the market even higher.

It is risky to try to trade these reversals, because if you get it wrong, you are certain to lose money. These incorrect signals are called "head fakes," which means that when the market is going in one direction, just as you buy (or sell stocks short), it fakes you out by suddenly going in the opposite direction.

For example, traders looking for a quick profit or investors who get caught up in the excitement of a rising market might buy into a fast-moving market. Minutes after they press the Enter key, the market reverses direction and plunges. It takes experience to know when to time the market, and most people get it wrong. It is less risky to wait until you're sure of the market direction.

Although investors are technically timing the market using some of these strategies, you are not trying to time the exact top or bottom, which is nearly impossible. Instead, you are entering or exiting the market when your indicators or clues say it's appropriate to do so. You may not be first to get out, but if you can save the majority of your portfolio (or lock in the majority of your profits), then you can consider that a success.

Market Mastery

A note for short-sellers: If the market is moving higher on high volume, do not attempt to short at the top. Too many short sellers, thinking the market can't go any higher, trade against a strong bull market and get wiped out. It is far safer to wait until the rally fails and drops on higher volume before you even think of shorting.

When Market Indicators Say Sell

With experience, and by following the previous signs, you should get a better feel for the overall market. The following handful of market indicators discussed will also help you understand when to exit a market that is turning south (downward). Note that we've already discussed some of these indicators. All we're doing here is investigating what to do when the market starts moving in the opposite direction.

- *Moving Averages:* If the S&P 500 or other major index falls (and stays) below its 50-day, 100-day, or 200-day moving averages, this is a bearish signal. Many investors watch moving averages, especially the 200-day, so a drop below is a bearish signal. Does it mean that you should immediately sell? No, but it's a significant clue that the time to sell is approaching. Keep in mind that moving averages is a lagging indicator, which means that its signals are often late.
- *Moving Average Convergence/Divergence (MACD):* MACD is also very popular with traders and investors. When MACD crosses below its 9-day signal line or below the zero line (and stays below), that is a bearish signal. As always, you must confirm with other indicators and your own analysis before buying or selling based on MACD. Like moving averages, MACD is a lagging indicator, so its signals are sometimes late.
- *Relative Strength Index (RSI):* RSI tells you whether the market index is overbought or oversold. Unfortunately, RSI can remain overbought or oversold for a long time before the index reverses direction. Nevertheless, it's useful in pointing out when the market is getting a bit frothy or too complacent.
- *The Bond Market:* Keep your eye on the 10-year Treasury yield (Symbol: ^TNX). When the yield rises, then bond

prices are falling. When the yield drops, bond prices are rising. If the yield moves up too quickly, and bond prices fall, it not only hurts the bond market but it may disrupt the stock market.

- *P/E Ratio of the S&P 500:* Historically, the average P/E of the S&P 500 is 15. If the P/E of the market is well above 15, the market may be overbought. However, if the P/E of the S&P 500 is below 15, the market could be oversold. Remember, the market can remain overbought or oversold (according to the P/E) for long periods before reversing direction.

- *Chart Patterns:* If the bull market is really coming to an end, you may see chart patterns such as a double top. This is a pattern in which a stock rises to point X, declines, and once again rallies to the same level (X). Then there is a final decline. In other words, the stock rose to the same level twice but failed to break through to the upside.

- *The Market:* The most powerful indicator is the market itself. It is always right, and always has the final word. The market performance, represented by the major market indexes, should be viewed on a chart. (If you're new to the market, charts can be found on your brokerage firm's website, Google Finance, Yahoo! Finance, or StockCharts.com.)

Make a point to view the overall market regularly (short-term traders look it at all day, but once a week is adequate for most investors). Your goal is to identify the market trend, and determine when the current trend appears to be ending, and if a new one is starting.

Market Mastery

Although market indicators are powerful tools, they do not provide magic answers. They only help to determine which way the market trend is going. Every brokerage firm as well as major financial websites will have charts and indicators. Again, use indicators in conjunction with your own observation and analysis. Keep in mind that although indicators are helpful tools, they are not perfect, and sometimes give false signals.

What Should You Do Next?

Let's say that you look at technical and sentiment indicators and believe that the bull market is on its last legs. Be careful. Although the bulls are no longer running, you may not be seeing the start of a bear market. After all, the market can go sideways for a long time before it turns downward. Along the way, it can have many fits and starts, giving hope to both the bulls and bears.

If you believe the bull market is ending, it is usually a mistake to make an aggressive bearish trade (such as shorting or buying inverse ETFs, which are discussed in Chapter 10). If you sell stocks short too early, even though you may be proven right eventually, you may lose so much money before the direction changes that you will be forced out of your positions.

Whenever you feel the urge to make a fast trade, remember that often the smartest move of all is sitting tight. There is nothing more aggravating than being right about the market's direction and still losing money. If you buy too early near the end of a bear market or if you sell short too early near the end of a bull market, you'll suffer financially.

Don't Panic

If you see evidence that the bull market is ending, don't panic. There is no urgency because few will believe that you are correct. Check the indicators to see if you notice a trend change. Short-term traders may sell on these signals, but long-term investors require more evidence.

Don't rely only on the technical indicators, but don't ignore them, either. If you determine from the indicators and your analysis of the overall market that the bull market is definitely over and that you must do something, be sure you are not selling for emotional reasons. If you believe you are taking action because of fear rather than hard evidence, then reconsider. (You can always sell part of your position.) Nevertheless, financier Bernard Baruch, when asked how he became so wealthy at such a young age, responded: "I made my money by selling too soon." Sometimes it's best to be safe rather than sorry.

Get Out Slowly or Quickly, but Get Out

We'll assume that you've completed your analysis and that, based on what the indicators reveal, it's clear to you that the market is turning bearish and you must exit your positions. What should you do?

There are a number of sell strategies you can use. First, you can pyramid out (i.e., scale out of your positions). Start by unloading a portion of the shares of your index ETF (or stock position). You want to sell down to the boring point, that is, where you no longer lose sleep because of what you own.

As we've discussed, a bull market can end with a bang or a whimper. Sometimes a bull market will end and go sideways for a long time. At other times, it goes directly into a bear market. If it ends with a whimper or goes sideways, you have time to scale out.

Only you can decide whether to get out quickly or slowly, but when it's the right time, get out and don't look back.

If you exit too early, you will miss out on potential gains—but you will sleep soundly. If you get out too late, you will lose money. It's not easy to sell at the right time, but by following the indicators, you have a better-than-average chance of doing the right thing at an appropriate time.

If the bull market ends with a bang—that is, a crash—you have a choice to make. Assuming you missed an opportunity to sell, you can grit your teeth, try to ride out the crash, and hope that it doesn't last long. If possible, however, try to escape early without too much damage. (If you can escape a market crash of more than 20 percent with less than 5 percent in losses, you did well.)

One thing to keep in mind: History says that some very rapid black swan events (such as a *flash crash*) can end as quickly as they began. If what's occurring looks like a black swan event, the odds are good it won't last long.

Market Mastery

There have been times in stock market history when everything (technical and sentiment indicators) lined up perfectly, and anyone who took the time to look could see that the bull market was ending. At other times, it hasn't been as obvious, and the market was very volatile before ending.

Since there are no easy answers, once again, you must use your observational skills to determine the status of the bull market. Few people can do it accurately or consistently, but if you can correctly predict the market direction more than 55 percent of the time, consider that a victory.

Here is what Jesse Livermore said in *Reminiscences of a Stock Operator* about managing the end of a bull market:

"Disregarding the big swing and trying to jump in and out was fatal to me. Nobody can catch all the fluctuations. In a bull market your game is to buy and hold until you believe that the bull market is near its end. To do this you must study general conditions and not tips or special factors affecting individual stocks. Then get out of all your stocks: get out for keeps! Wait until you see, or if you prefer, until you think you see, the turn of the

market; the beginning of the reversal of general conditions. You have to use your brains and your vision to do this; otherwise my advice would be as idiotic as to tell you to buy cheap and sell dear."

In the next chapter, you will learn about booms, busts, and bubbles.

CHAPTER 6

Booms, Busts, and Bubbles

While all bull markets eventually come to an end, either by turning sideways or by turning into a bear market, a unique phenomenon occurs with some bull markets. Instead of coming to a peaceful end and running out of gas, they actually go higher. Much higher. If they go high enough (and that cannot be calculated until afterward), they can become a bubble.

What Goes Up Must Come Down

There is nothing more fascinating than a market bubble. The market reaches heights that seem unimaginable, rising well above technical levels, and blowing through fundamentals such as P/E ratios as if they were meaningless.

As the bubble gets bigger, the market rises so high and so fast that it will shock investors and financial commentators. Those who are fully invested are euphoric, and many believe they are stock-picking geniuses.

Other investors, who look around to see how much money everyone else is making, jump into the market, attempting to get rich fast. Anyone who has bet against the market (i.e., short sellers) has probably given up. Some even change sides and go long. During these times, Wall Street goes mad. It's as if everyone is afflicted with a psychosis called "bubblemania."

During these extraordinary times, when it is too easy to make money in the stock market, wise investors move to the sidelines. Although it's difficult to resist a free handout, the longer the mania continues, the harder the market will fall—and the fall will come.

When Wall Street Enters the Bubble Zone

As the bubble forms, fund managers can't buy stocks fast enough, using cash that latecomers are sending. Some investors are using margin to buy more stock (and margin debt levels start to spike). Although some detect there is a bubble, most people don't believe it. Almost everyone, pros and retail investors, think they can exit before the bubble bursts. Many, including the Fed and some of Wall Street's brightest analysts, don't even see a bubble.

That's why bubbles are so fascinating. You seldom realize you're in one until it pops.

One of the earliest and most notorious bubbles occurred in the mid-seventeenth century in Holland. It involved, of all things, tulips. In 1637 Dutch townsfolk were buying and selling rare tulip bulbs called "bizarres" for prices as high as $200,000 (using today's prices). Many people became rich . . . before they went broke.

Most of you are familiar with the 1929 bubble (and crash). In the 1990s we saw another bubble in the tech sector: People couldn't buy Internet stocks fast enough; they bid up stocks such as Pets.com, Webvan.com, and other dot-coms to obscene price levels. You could buy anything with .com after its name and make a fortune, sometimes within days. One clue that the market had reached bubble territory was the number of people who quit their jobs to become full-time day traders.

In 2000, the bubble burst. Many companies collapsed, while others saw their stock prices take huge hits. A lot of those former day traders scrambled to find new jobs.

The housing bubble of 2007 that preceded the Great Recession was similar. When regular folks started quitting their jobs to day trade stocks or flip houses, this was a huge red flag. Many people were collecting houses as if they were baseball cards, and books about getting rich in real estate (and the stock market) were bestsellers. Then, in the fall of 2008, it came crashing down.

The confusing thing about bubbles is they can last so long that people no longer believe they're bubbles. The ultra-high stock prices and valuations appear normal, as if they have reached a permanent plateau.

When you're looking at the bubble from the outside, it may seem as if the whole world has gone mad. Still, it's hard to resist participating in the market when your neighbors seem to be getting rich. Everyone on Wall Street is celebrating as the prices of individual stocks are doubling and tripling. Those who warn of a crash are ridiculed. The media starts running stories of average people making a paper fortune buying any "old thing."

Market Mastery

Not every bull market turns into a bubble, but every bubble is created during a bull market. You can have a healthy bull market built on solid earnings, strong economic conditions, and good financial policies. This will also cause the market to go higher.

But if the stock market goes higher primarily on speculation, on the idea that prices will keep going higher—not because of good earnings or economic conditions but on rampant speculation—then you may have the makings of a bubble.

When the market is in the early stages of a bubble, at first it feels like a strong bull market. As the unstoppable market soars higher, even those who are suspicious of the market are awed by its power. Smart bears, after all, don't dare bet against the market.

As the bubble grows and matures, the financial world becomes euphoric. Bull markets are exciting, but bubbles are intoxicating. It's hard for anyone to identify, or even admit, that the market is in a bubble because it feels so good. No one wants to get out—they'll miss out on all those delicious unrealized profits. So almost everyone stays in.

Every bubble is different, but the one common characteristic is that prices soar to heights that in retrospect seem ridiculously high, even if at the time they didn't appear excessive. Partly because of this, it takes a tremendous amount of strength and confidence to avoid investing in a bubble.

Lessons from 1929

When another bubble forms in the future (and it's guaranteed to happen), you'd do well to learn from history. In 1928, a young stockbroker, Charles Merrill (who had also survived the 1907 crash), recognized that stock prices had gone too high. When he told his friends that he was thinking of selling his stocks, they urged him to see a psychiatrist. After all, anyone who sold stocks when the market is going up must be crazy, right?

After a session with the psychiatrist, both Merrill and the doctor agreed that stocks had gotten too high. Together they went to their broker's offices and sold their stocks. They realized that amid all the madness around them, they were the only sane ones (a decision that saved their portfolios). By the way, Merrill later founded the brokerage firm Merrill Lynch, presumably with the money he didn't lose in the market.

Here's another story. A few months before the 1929 crash, a young stockbroker wrote the following:

"The exciting markets continue and these four million day sessions have gradually become an accepted fact. It would seem that those who are guiding the fortunes of this record-breaking

market, pick a handful of new favorites each day and thus far have been successful in attaining the objective they set out to reach. Wall Street is literally full of rumors and one can hear almost anything about any stock on the list.

"Just where the boiling market will end is anyone's guess. On one hand, it is believed that stocks have been well distributed and that they are in the hands of the public and that the market has been carried up to unreasonably and to dangerous heights by an inflamed public imagination.

"On the other hand, many shrewd judges of the market do not believe anything of the sort and expect to see the market quiet down and the railroad and oil shares which have taken but little part in the demonstration will be the next favorites, while the industrials take a long rest."

The author was my grandfather, Charles, who wrote this analysis for his firm, Charles Sincere & Company. If it was possible to go back in time, I'd like to ask him if he thought the market had reached unsustainable levels.

It's interesting that "shrewd judges of the market" had no clue that a bubble was forming. Even the smartest, most famous, and wealthiest investors can be completely wrong. Although a few on the fringe warned of an inflated market, the overwhelming majority believed that the bull market would continue indefinitely. By the time the crowd realized the market was really in a bubble, it was too late.

Throughout history, very shrewd people have made terrible predictions, many of which were overly optimistic. Few will forget the book title, *Dow 36,000*, which was released in 1999, two years before the market crashed. Likewise, historians will never let renowned economist Irving Fisher forget his words: "Stock prices have reached what looks like a permanently high plateau." He uttered this three days before the 1929 stock market crash. This untimely prediction ruined his reputation.

Bottom Line

Just because someone is smart and famous doesn't mean he is always right. On the other hand, if you believe you're in the middle of a bubble, don't forget these words by British economist John Maynard Keynes: "The market can stay irrational longer than you can stay solvent."

Don't Bet Against a Bubble

Although the easiest solution to a bubble is to move to cash, it is not a comfortable decision. After all, you appear to be missing out on the opportunity of a lifetime. All of your friends are getting rich—at least on paper—and they will question your sanity.

You might even be tempted to start shorting. Don't make that mistake! The market can still go higher. When investors believe there is little or no risk in investing in the market, when speculation is rampant, when it appears that everyone else is on another planet, wait until the financial world comes back to earth. If you short too early, you could lose your shirt.

To survive, you need to manage risk as well as your positions. At first, sit and wait. If you truly believe there is a bubble, don't participate. Even though you're not making money now, there will be other opportunities in the future. Consider this a rule: Do not trade stocks that appear to be in a bubble.

Blowing Bubbles

Following are signs that a bubble is forming in the market (and don't forget that despite all of these warning signs, the market can continue to go much higher; after all, it's a bubble).

- Retail investors are pouring money into stock mutual funds, which are reaching all-time highs. Instead of panic selling, there is a buying stampede as investors are anxious to buy before the price of their mutual funds or stocks go even higher. (It's the fear of missing out that causes a full-fledged panic to get into stocks.)
- At investing conferences, crowds of professional money managers are super bullish and don't believe the market is in any danger. When both clients and money managers believe that stocks are only going in one direction (up), this is a huge red flag, an indication that a bubble is forming.
- Long-time professional bears have given up and turned bullish. Another warning signal.
- Sentiment readings from AAII and Investors Intelligence are over 70 or 75 percent.
- Investors believe the Fed will protect them by printing money, thereby keeping interest rates low indefinitely. When market participants believe that it's easy to get rich, that is a danger sign.
- Certain technology stocks have reached all-time highs, and many are going higher, some with little or no earnings. When momentum stocks go sky high based on no current or future earnings, that is a huge red flag.
- Margin levels (investors are borrowing money to buy more stocks) are reaching extreme levels.

- Some fundamental stock valuations are so high that there are few bargains, and value investors can't find anything cheap to buy.
- The stock market has reached all-time highs, and has zoomed up by double digits year to date.
- Other asset classes are acting strangely. For example, the yield on the 10-year Treasury is spiking, and bonds are falling fast along with gold.

Pop Goes the Bubble

The amazing thing about bubbles is that most people believe they can get out in time. In fact, when a bubble pops, everything goes down at once. The rush to buy will suddenly become a rush to sell, and the exit door will be crowded.

There are a number of clues before the market weakens and the bubble bursts. For example, some of the strongest stocks in the indexes begin to fall. At the market close, there is high-volume selling. Although the market ignored bad news while it was going up, it is suddenly selling off even on good news.

Unfortunately, all bubbles end the same way, with a gigantic pop. At this point, the market can suddenly crash, which means investors have no chance to escape. If they're lucky, the market will fizzle before it crashes, offering them a little escape time. Too often, though, this isn't the case.

As the market weakens, at first there is disbelief. In the early stages, nervous investors in stock mutual funds believe their fund managers will protect them. As the market continues to fall and the losses mount, panicked investors suddenly realize the market is not coming back anytime soon. Many will sell their stock positions and mutual funds before they lose more money. When everyone runs for the exits at once, the market falls faster and further. By now, there is "blood in the street."

Greed pushed the market higher and now it's fear that drives stocks lower. The scariest part is that no one knows how low the market can go. As the market crashes, hope turns to despair, and few people have the desire to buy. Don't forget: Once the market reaches bubble territory and pops, it is almost impossible to sell in time.

Bubbles Never End Well

In the future, stock-trading technology will improve, but one thing that never changes is human nature. As long as there is a stock market, there will be booms, busts, and bubbles. All you can do is step back and look for the clues.

Nevertheless, when the market goes up too far and fast, when investors believe that they are protected from downturns and that risk has been eliminated, you know it will not end well. People sometimes forget that the stock market is not a money market account, or an ATM. When they forget those facts, the market always teaches them a lesson. It would be nice to say it's one they should never forget, but they always do.

In the next chapter, you will learn how to prepare for a worst-case scenario.

CHAPTER 7

Prepare for Market Crashes

Going through a crash is eerily similar to watching a car wreck. You can't believe what you are seeing. When the market declines as much as 20 percent in a few days, it's an "official" crash. The news will be featured on many television reports. The financial commentators may seem stunned and are sometimes angry that investors are selling. They tell listeners not to panic (good advice), but they look panicked.

Bullish financial analysts will also tell their clients to stay calm. They may even try to sell their clients on the idea that this decline is only temporary, that this is a great buying opportunity. Bearish analysts will tell you why the market is crashing (and remind you that they saw it coming, and that they tried to warn you). Don't fall for any of it. Use your clues, observations, and analysis to decide what to do next.

Nothing makes investors more nervous than the possibility of a crash. In the financial markets, it's the worst possible outcome because you can lose everything. Even saying that the market might crash evokes strong feelings.

That is why every week, someone writes an article about a possible crash. The higher the market goes, the more articles appear. And if the market goes in the opposite direction (lower), crash predictions also increase. In other words, at market extremes, there are many crash warnings.

Technical analysts often see crash patterns, and invent cool names for indicators such as the Hindenburg Omen (which sounds really scary). They eagerly warn their readers that a crash is imminent.

Rarely do any of these predictions come true. No one can consistently predict where the market will go next, and that includes a stock market crash. Crash predictions are usually made by people trying to gain some fame for themselves, and are often worthless. You might as well try your luck on the roulette wheel.

Although crash predictions should be ignored, you can identify clues that a correction or pullback is near; better yet, you can tell when the market is in dangerous territory. While you don't want to be so petrified by fear of a severe decline that you refuse to invest, you also want to know when the market is getting overbought or unsafe.

In this chapter, we'll take a closer look at crashes, and how you can prepare for them. Most of the time, their precise timing is impossible to predict, but if you are alert to market conditions, you can identify some of the danger signs.

Understanding Market Crashes

A crash occurs when the market undergoes a sudden and intense decline. Technically, there is no precise percentage for it to be defined as a crash, but most analysts agree that anything between 15 to 20 percent qualifies. The October 1929 crash (in which the market initially fell by over 23 percent in two days) and the 22 percent crash in October 1987 are two examples. (Now you know why investors get nervous in October!)

Crashes can be isolated events or they can be catalysts for bear markets. In other words, you can technically have a crash without a bear market. On the other hand, some crashes occur as the market has already entered bear territory and is in a downtrend.

The reason investors fear crashes is that there is little time to exit their positions. Although a bear market may go down by higher amounts than a crash, at least you have a chance to get out on the way down. With crashes, you are trapped.

To protect yourself from a crash, you must prepare in advance. The people who suffer the most during a crash employ one or more of these strategies:

1. Go on margin (borrowing money from your brokerage firm to buy stocks)
2. Use speculative strategies such as selling naked put options.

     Advanced note: Selling naked (or uncovered) puts allows you to purchase shares of stock. In the hands of an experienced trader, it is a strategic way of purchasing stock at a discount. In the hands of a novice, misuse of this strategy gives options a bad name. In a worst-case scenario, if the stock price falls sharply, the novice's account will be destroyed. There are excellent option strategies to use during a bear market, but this is not one of them.
3. Own extremely speculative technology stocks
4. Own 100 percent individual stocks (without being diversified into other investments)

If you are using any of these strategies, it will be difficult to survive a severe market crash. People who use most of these strategies are usually wiped out when the market collapses. Even a pullback or correction can cause pain if you use one of these strategies.

Bottom Line

Don't go on margin (unless you're an experienced pro), don't sell naked options, and—most important—diversify. If you own an index ETF or index fund, you will be diversified, and although you will take a hit in a crash, the damage probably won't be severe enough to wipe you out completely. In fact, the reason buying index funds is less risky than buying individual stocks is that during a true market crash, the indexes will fall, but many stocks will fall further and faster. Being diversified in index funds helps reduce the pain (although that also depends on the stocks you own).

Market Pullbacks and Corrections

Market pullbacks occur fairly often, and they are usually healthy, helping to form a base for the next bull market rally. After all, if there were no pullbacks, the market would go straight up, and that would be unrealistic and dangerous. Corrections are more severe and can be harmful to the value of your portfolio. Fortunately, they usually don't last very long. Many market experts believe that corrections are also healthy, and are needed for a bull market to keep rising.

Market Mastery

When the market declines by more than 10 percent, it is considered a correction. The term "bear market" is typically not used unless the decline exceeds 20 percent for a sustained time period. Don't worry too much about the precise definitions. Your task is to know when to be invested and when to be on the sidelines.

Bottom Line

Pullbacks and corrections may temporarily hurt, but don't cause long-lasting pain. A crash or bear market, on the other hand, causes severe damage to the economy and the stock market.

Not all crashes are as severe as 1929 or 2008. Here are some less significant types of crashes.

The Flash Crash

A "flash crash" is a phenomenon in which the market unexpectedly plunges. It occurs very rapidly, in hours or even minutes. It is an aberration that is quickly corrected once traders get over their fears. As soon as people determine that there was no rationale for the rapid decline, buyers reappear and push prices back to earlier levels.

One flash crash occurred on May 6, 2010 (the infamous "fat finger" trade), which caused a short-term panic. Reportedly, either a high-speed trader inadvertently pressed the wrong button or there was a computer glitch. The Dow plunged 1,000 points (approximately 9 percent) and then, within fifteen minutes, bounced back to its previous value.

During the May 2010 flash crash, bidders went into hiding and for some stocks there were no bids higher than $.01 per share. Although it is difficult to believe, some unfortunate people who entered an order to "sell at the market" received that one penny price. Buyers were surprised, and sellers were horrified at the huge losses. Some of the most outrageous trades were busted (i.e., canceled by the exchanges), but many traders who had entered perfectly reasonable stop loss market orders were shocked at the prices they received when selling their stocks. Fortunately, flash crashes are quite rare, and once the cause of the decline is discovered and fixed, the market quickly bounces back.

Black Swans

Sometimes an unpredictable and unexpected event sends the market indexes reeling; such occurrences are called "black swans" because of their rarity. These random financial catastrophes cannot be anticipated, but the markets react to the news immediately.

In the past, black swan events included terrorist attacks, a currency crisis, or spikes in interest rates.

Can you predict a black swan? To be defined as a black swan, it has to be an unforeseeable event. Therefore, the answer is no.

Market Mastery

Don't lose sleep over black swans; it's impossible to predict the unpredictable. Nevertheless, once you have experienced a black swan crash, see if the market bounces back quickly or if the event is the catalyst for a bear market. Although you cannot protect yourself against a black swan, you can get out in time to avoid a severe bear market. If you already own bearish positions such as protective put options or inverse ETFs (which will be discussed in Chapter 10), you will feel less pain from the effects of a black swan.

Technical Clues That a Correction or Crash Is Near

After a market crash, it's easy to look back and find out what happened. In fact, experts will tell you a dozen different reasons why the market plunged. Sadly, that doesn't help if you've already lost over 20 percent of your portfolio.

Crashes don't occur often, so the clues generated are not always noticeable. Even when you do see clues, they may not seem important until later, when the damage has already been done.

The following clues are ideas to consider when forming your market forecast. As you learn to be a market observer, you may discover other signs. After all, being a market analyst is similar to being a detective, which means you often rely on circumstantial evidence to make your case.

The hard part is determining which evidence is important, and which is not. You should look for evidence and leads on financial websites such as Bloomberg, MarketWatch, Google Finance, Yahoo!

Finance, Reuters, and Associated Press (to name only a few). The news media is usually your best resource for monitoring the pulse of the financial world, but be very careful to separate facts from opinion when reading.

Here are a few clues that a correction or crash is looming. The list is short because crashes are so unexpected, although they usually occur in a dangerous market environment. Corrections, however, are easier to identify.

- The market has dropped below its 200-day moving average. Other technical weaknesses, such as the market moving below support levels, may also occur. While the buy-on-the-dippers might claim that the pullback is a "great buying opportunity," do not be persuaded. Too often, it is financial suicide to buy on the way down.
- More stocks are making new 52-week lows and keep falling on higher volume.
- At the end of the some trading days, there are strong selloffs on high volume. Even more revealing, if the market starts off strong, but sells off at the end of the day, that is a significant negative signal. Those failed rallies and intraday reversals on high volume are significant. Perhaps the market won't crash, but it will probably be in for a rough ride in the near future.
- In a bear market, the potential for a significant crash or correction increases.

Crashes Rarely Happen at the Top

Many people are surprised to learn that most crashes do not occur when the market is at its top. Therefore, if the market is rising like a rocket, breaking through resistance and trading above its moving averages, it is very unlikely to suddenly reverse direction and crash.

As long as the move to higher levels is accompanied by higher volume, the chances of a sharp reversal are minimal. Of course, there will always be exceptions, but based on history, markets usually pull back after failed rallies, or after a series of weak closes (lower lows and lower highs on a chart).

However, if the market rises fast and hard (goes parabolic), and then is unable to move higher after the first pullback, this is a warning signal that another pullback may be imminent.

If the market shows signs of turning from bullish to bearish with increasing volume, an environment for a possible correction or crash has been created. A crash is most likely when the market is already on the way *down*, not on the way up.

Market Mastery

After the crash, it doesn't help you to dwell on why the market crashed. That's old news. Now you must focus on doing the opposite of everyone else, and looking for buying opportunities.

What Should You Do During a Crash?

As the market continues to fall, many analysts tell investors to stay put and not panic. Some advisors even urge their clients to buy more shares of stock. That is the opposite of my message to you. As you observe more bearish signals, you should be scaling back more of your holdings. In the event of a crash, ideally you will have no more long (i.e., bullish) investments.

As you know from the previous chapter, the probability of a crash increases when the market is in a bubble, but usually few recognize the bubble until after it pops. Crashes can occur without warning, leading to the next bear market. Even more confusing, crashes can also occur in the middle of a bear market.

Rather than panicking during or after a bear market, take a step back and analyze what happened. If what you saw was a black swan, more than likely the markets will bounce back quickly.

On the other hand, if the bear market took a long time to progress before the crash, there could be a severe economic crisis, and it might take months or years to recover. Even after the bear has departed, the bull may not arrive for a long time.

If you were prepared in advance (and I'm hoping this book will help), then you will see the bear market as a buying opportunity. On the other hand, don't buy too soon. First, wait for the market to stabilize before stepping back into it. Of course, rely on your clues and indicators.

What Happens after a Market Crash?

Although every market crash is different, we know what's happened in the past and can learn from it. There will be rallies and pullbacks after a crash, and a lot of volatility. Remember that some signals will be false, so do not expect to make a winning decision every time. Observe the market and act according to the message (charts, clues, and indicators) that it sends.

If you were prepared for the crash, then you have already taken defensive measures such as diversifying into cash, bonds or commodities. Although that will help, it may not be enough. After all, during a crash, most asset classes lose value.

If you do get caught in a crash, do not panic. If there is a trend change, you must also be willing to change your market opinion.

Often a steep decline is followed by one of two occurrences: more steep declines or the formation of a bottom. It will take some clear-headed analysis to determine which scenario is more likely. If losses are manageable (less than 10 percent of your portfolio), you still have time to cut your losses, or scale back your long positions. There is no right answer since every crash is unique.

During chaotic financial periods, it's essential that you keep a clear mind and focus on the facts. Do not succumb to the hysteria—and there will be a lot of it. This is not the time to make impulsive investments.

Many people will be angry at the stock market for a long time. Others will be afraid to invest in the market again, and may have already moved to cash. Stock market crashes make many people afraid and distrustful, and it's understandable. At the time, it seems as if the lost money can never be recovered. It's similar to the way people feel after a drunken hangover: bleary-eyed, tired, and exhausted. After losing money, it is common to feel vulnerable.

If you are still holding stocks or mutual funds, you may be tempted to sell everything. It doesn't help when the media warns of more bad times ahead. It's easy to succumb to fear, but you must resist that urge. Do a quick but thorough analysis. If the market is still above its moving averages (and support levels) and is giving a bullish signal, then do not sell in a panic. (If you are afraid and feel that you must do something to reduce risk, you can always scale back by selling some of your investments.)

Nevertheless, if your indicators and analysis signal a bear market, it is time to make a graceful exit. This doesn't mean selling everything at the market immediately. You also don't want to rely only on the hope that the market rallies so you can recover losses. Follow your bear market investment plan, which includes scaling out of your long positions.

In the next chapter I'll discuss the characteristics and strategies of sideways markets. As you'll learn, they can be challenging.

CHAPTER 8

Characteristics and Strategies of a Sideways Market

Not many people like a sideways market, and it's easy to understand why. A sideways market can be dangerous and unpredictable, but it can also be flat and boring. When a market goes sideways, the bears and bulls fight for control, and it can take months or longer before a winner is declared. Sometimes, after a lengthy bull market, a market may go sideways before turning into a bear market.

Bullish analysts say that the market is "consolidating"—that is, taking a rest before going higher again. There is nothing wrong with this point of view, and in fact they could be right. Some cautious bears, however, may wait safely on the sidelines until a winner is declared (bull or bear). Those with a bearish view generally believe the sideways market will end badly.

Investing in or trading a sideways market is extremely challenging, and is frustrating for both the bulls and bears. The bears are unhappy because the market doesn't go down low enough to make a profit. The bulls are unhappy because the market stops going straight up and begins to meander around.

A sideways market is an indecisive one. Once you identify a sideways market, think of whether the previous trend was bullish or bearish. If it follows a lengthy bull market, a bear market could be near, but it's not guaranteed.

A sideways market can occur at any time and last for months, sometimes years. Often it will appear at the end of a trend. For example, if there is a strong bull market that is coming to an end, instead of moving into a bear market, the market may go sideways for a long period.

A sideways market that occurs during a bull market can be dangerous. More than likely, it means that the bull market is coming to an end, but it takes time to know for sure. It's also possible for the market to go sideways, then continue moving up (consolidation). In that case, the bull market will resume.

During a sideways market, the bulls and bears appear to be having a tug of war with no clear winner—at first. It's essential that you don't become impatient. Often the smartest move you can make is to sit and wait. In fact, the biggest mistake you can make is to try to force profits. That is a sure way of losing money.

There are two main types of sideways markets: volatile and flat. During a flat sideways market, volume is low, and few market participants want to commit new money to the market. It's as if the entire market has been put to sleep.

The volatile sideways market is more exciting and offers more trading opportunities, but it still goes nowhere. Let's analyze this more closely.

The Volatile Sideways Market

The volatile sideways market is a difficult market to trade. It churns a lot but basically ends approximately where it started. A sideways market trades between support and resistance, never breaking through to the upside or downside. Sometimes, the market makes extreme moves, only to reverse the next day.

During a volatile sideways market, the market reacts to any breaking news, perhaps a Fed announcement or an earnings report.

Since there is nothing to move the market, the market will latch on to any news, hoping for a market-moving event.

Investors generally don't like volatile sideways markets because the market acts like a roller coaster. During the day or throughout the week, there can be multiple market reversals, confusing investors. (On the other hand, some traders like a volatile market because it's so easy to find short-term buy and sell signals.)

Strategies for a Volatile Sideways Market

Volatile sideways markets are risky for both bulls and bears. The safest and most conservative strategy during such a market is to increase your cash position and stay on the sidelines without committing much money. By waiting until the sideways market ends, you can choose the only side that matters: the right side (which will be known later).

Trying to make money during a sideways market is best left to the pros or short-term traders. Investors can sit tight until the sideways market ends, but you must be prepared to get out of long positions if the market starts to sell off.

Although having a sizeable cash position during a volatile sideways market is the safest strategy, you don't want to be in cash indefinitely. Too many fearful investors stay in cash too long and then miss out on the next bull market. On the other hand, if the sideways market turns bearish, you will be pleased that you had a large cash position.

Bottom Line

The volatile sideways market could go either way, so staying on the sidelines, in cash, is often the safest move. If you're a long-term investor, you can still keep your index ETFs and index funds, but reducing exposure to the market during a sideways market is prudent.

The Flat Sideways Market

In a flat sideways market, the market also goes nowhere but without the excitement of a volatile environment. There are few buyers or sellers. Jesse Livermore discussed the frustration of a sideways market by quoting one of his trader acquaintances: "It was the kind of market where not even a skunk could make a scent."

In this type of situation, the market could go sideways for months, or in extreme cases for years. When not even a skunk can make a scent, you know it won't be easy to produce profits. (Livermore often went fishing during sideways markets.)

To survive a flat sideways market, most of all you need patience. The last thing you want to do is to buy something, anything, hoping for a profit. In a boring sideways market, only patient investors will be rewarded. During this kind of market, you should cut back on share size and not make huge investments until the bull market returns. Once you can identify a new trend, you can invest more heavily.

If you're a stock picker, this is a good time to find unloved stocks with upside potential. If the sideways market turns bullish, finding a "diamond in the rough" can bring a good payoff in the future. Hopefully you won't have to wait too long for the sideways market to end. Just be ready when it happens.

Bottom Line

Wait for a better opportunity to make money. The market has a certain ebb and flow, so patiently wait for it to reveal its hand. If you try to force something to happen, you will probably lose money.

Market Mastery

Be sure to check out trading volume in a sideways market. Typically, volume will be low because enthusiasm for the market is waning.

Strategies for a Flat Sideways Market

Following are a few strategies you can consider during a flat sideways market.

Cash or Cash Equivalents (CDs and Money Markets)

It's a good time to contemplate cash equivalents such as a money market account or alternative investments such as bonds or commodities. First, check current interest rates. If these are high enough to produce a return that is acceptable to you (perhaps 4 or 5 percent to start), consider fixed income products including money market funds or CDs. These investments may outperform stocks during some market conditions.

On the other hand, if interest rates are low and going lower, then buying bonds is a good choice. Bonds tend to do well in low-interest-rate environments. If rates are rising, however, then bond funds are not recommended. Hint: Check the 10-year Treasury for the current yield.

Index Funds

You can hold your index ETF or index fund during a flat sideways market, but don't expect to make a fortune. Those who see evidence that the market might take a turn for the worse can reduce positions. Don't forget that the market can go either way after it's done going sideways.

Selling Covered Calls

Another strategy that can work in a sideways market is writing covered calls on stocks you own (if you own any). In a nutshell, that strategy includes selling the right to buy your stock at a specific price to another investor. The other party pays you a cash premium in return for the right to temporarily own your stock. Put another way, you receive cash up front for selling the rights to your stock. In a way, you are renting out your stocks to option buyers, and they pay you cash for the privilege. As long as the market is not sinking, this strategy can bring in extra income. Additional details are required to gain a complete understanding of this strategy.

When a Sideways Market Ends

If there is a long, boring sideways market, you must be on the lookout for signs that it is finally ending. If it's consolidating, it may turn into a bull market after weeks, months, or years. If the sideways market came after a bear market or crash, then the odds are it will eventually turn bullish. On the other hand, if the sideways market occurs after a lengthy bull market, it could turn into a bear market.

Finding a good buying opportunity takes experience, and that is the reason why we do not rush into making trades. It is difficult to get the timing right, so at least wait for the bulk of the evidence (clues) to dictate a trading opportunity before committing too heavily. Be willing to miss the start of a big rally, as long as you don't miss all of it. The challenging part is that every market is different, so it's difficult to make specific rules about when is the best time to buy. That is one of the reasons why scaling into a position allows you to test buying opportunities.

In the next chapter, you'll learn about the characteristics of a bear market—that is, when the market generally goes down.

CHAPTER 9

Characteristics of a Bear Market

A bear market is a miserable experience for nearly everyone on Wall Street (except for short sellers or those in cash). Bear markets can be sleepy and dangerous, and the longer they continue, the more they sap the energy and enthusiasm from investors.

Go back to our metaphor about being on a boat in the middle of the ocean. Now imagine you see a coming storm. You put down your sails and get under cover. Your goal is to ride out the storm, to stay afloat until it passes. Like storms at sea, bear markets are inevitable, a natural part of the stock market cycle. They should be neither feared nor despised.

Where Have All the Buyers Gone?

As remarked before, when a bear market begins, most investors and nearly everyone on Wall Street are in denial. They don't want the good times to end, so they may buy every time the market dips. However, buying on the pullbacks, which worked during a bull market, fails when the market turns bearish. Instead of rallying and moving higher, the market falls and continues to go lower. Investors are surprised and disappointed.

After all, during the years of a bull market investors have gotten a little spoiled. Whenever the market fell, it always came back. Even when there was bad news, the market shrugged it off. Now, however, even good news is ignored, and the market continues to drop.

If you're in a true bear market—and it'll take some time to convince you and everyone else of that—the recovery may take a lot longer than the experts anticipate. As the market keeps going lower, financial firms may still deny that it's really a bear market, though they'll find this harder and harder to claim. They may try to convince their customers that the market is near a bottom and about to recover. It's best to ignore these predictions because they're self-serving.

If the market doesn't stop falling (it usually doesn't go straight down but is more like a jagged downturn), eventually pundits and analysts will recognize it as a bear market. At what point it becomes a bear market is really for the history books. Either way, you have two priorities: First, protect your assets; second, make a profit.

When a Bear Market Starts Slowly

Slow bear markets are the most difficult for investor psychology. If you're not careful to study the clues, you may not realize it's a bear market until most of the damage has been done. As the bear market continues to cause havoc, and stocks move lower, sellers begin to overwhelm buyers. Every rally is met with additional selling pressure.

When enough time goes by, the lack of enthusiasm by investors eventually turns to anxiety. If the market falls low enough, that anxiety often turns to fear, and there could be a crash.

As I mentioned earlier, bear markets tend to be shorter, lasting a few months to a year. There are exceptions (such as the 1929 bear market, which lasted three years). Obviously, anything is possible in the future.

Market Mastery
The difference between a crash and bear market is length of time. Crashes are a quick decline, while bear markets occur over a longer period.

Nevertheless, don't mistake a temporary pullback for a turning point in the market. Just because the market goes down a few days in a row doesn't make it a bear market. Also, the market usually rebounds quickly from a crash, but more slowly from a bear market.

Professional investors who buy and hold during a bear market have strong stomachs. Obviously, it's not fun to see a bear market shred their stock and index positions. But because they are pros, they hold their positions no matter how great the pain. Why? Because they believe in the stocks they own. They also know that a bear market is only temporary.

When a Bear Starts with a Bang

If a bear market starts with a severe, rapid decline, everyone is aware that something bad just happened. At first some investors will view the correction or crash as a buying opportunity and not as a bear market.

As an investor or trader, you should be more concerned with *what* is happening rather than why it happened. It is more important to pay attention to the clues rather than get caught up in the emotions. (And many investors will be extremely emotional.)

It's almost always impossible to predict crashes. A major international financial crisis in Asia or Europe, a credit crunch, a spike in interest rates, a currency crisis, a weak economy, a plunging dollar, a mistake by the Fed, or the start of what appears to be a major war—any of these can cause a crash. One seemingly harmless event might be the catalyst, but in a crash, like a house of cards, the whole deck falls down (i.e., the vast majority of stock prices tumbles).

Looking back, you can see a series of conditions, some of them short term, and some long term, that brought about the crash. For example, before the crash, you may remember seeing headlines such as "Problems Resurface." In other words, the problems that were buried have come back to haunt the market. In reality, they never went away; they were just ignored.

Now the market is in a hard selloff, perhaps 10 percent or more. Don't agonize if you didn't get out before this. The important question is what to do now. You must decide whether you should sell quickly to avoid more losses, or hold and hope that the market rebounds. Hope is not a good emotion to have during a crash (or a bear market). In fact, hope has no place in the vocabulary of any investor or trader.

You May Have One Chance to Escape

The market often gives those still holding long positions a window of opportunity to get out of a bear market before the real damage is done. Many people miss this chance. Instead of limiting their losses and taking a relatively small hit, they do nothing until losses exceed 30 or 40 percent.

Market Mastery

If you already lost more than 50 percent, your account has taken a severe hit. Consider it an educational experience, and perhaps you will act sooner next time. At this point you might as well grit your teeth and hold, but that is a decision only you can make. Write down the reasons why you lost money, and study the list. That way you'll lessen the chances it will happen again. No one rings a bell when it's time to get out of the market. You have to do your own work, and recognize on your own the proper time to exit.

It would be nice to know when a 5 percent loss will turn into a 50 percent disaster, or when that 5 percent loss will become a 3 percent gain a few days later. Unfortunately, there's no foolproof way to tell every time.

The best antidote against losing money in a downturn is to be aware of when a market is getting dangerous. You must always be aware of your market environment. If a 3 to 5 percent pullback occurs during a strong bull market, don't be too alarmed. If that same pullback occurs during a sideways market or a bear market, alarm bells should be going off.

Market Mastery

If you still have time to get out of the market, and your indicators and signals tell you to do so, then get out, and get out now. The key is getting out early, not late. If you can get out early without causing too much damage to your portfolio, then do so. If you react too late, then you must avoid selling at the bottom.

The Bear Market Continues

As the bear market continues, even disciplined investors become nervous and wonder if they should sell. The scary part is that no one can predict what is going to happen. Investors start worrying about worst-case scenarios.

Although it's true that the market always comes back, unfortunately it's also true, as many learned during the 1970s, that the market can meander around for years without moving significantly. Don't assume that what happened in the past will happen in the future. There are no guarantees.

As the market keeps dropping, some experts will continue to suggest that you buy on the dip. Don't listen to them. Conversely, others will claim that the market is headed for a massive crash. Don't listen to them, either. React to facts and figures, to the information you get from your charts and from your key indicators—not emotions.

Capitulation

Often during a bear market, many retail investors start off by buying and holding. As the market continues to fall, some of them panic. Although they were determined to hold on to their stocks and mutual funds, once losses reach 50 percent or more they can no longer take it. As the market continues to fall, the final stage occurs—capitulation: mass panic by sellers.

This is the point when investors collectively throw in the towel and get out, accepting any available price for their holdings. The pain becomes so great that they sell all of their positions, right at the bottom! In fact, one of the reasons that a bear market often ends so violently is the huge wave of people who suddenly sell. As mutual fund redemptions increase, and stocks are sold in a panic, stock prices are driven lower and lower.

Sadly, at this stage, almost all asset classes (bonds, commodities, emerging markets, etc.) fail, so there is no safe haven other than cash. When everything falls at once, most diversification formulas are nearly worthless.

Because retail investors are selling their mutual funds, money managers must sell stocks. This pressure adds to the stock market's woes and prices fall even further. It's a mad dash towards an exit door that is slowly closing. It's not easy to get out when everyone else has the same idea. At this point, people want out of the market at any price.

If you are on the sidelines watching, that final wave of capitulation is a signal that the market is nearing bottom. No one wants to unload a portfolio close to the bottom, but many do, because they're afraid their stocks and mutual funds are going to zero.

Others, who have held tightly to their investments on the way down, decide to keep holding no matter what. Many feel like sitting ducks. (All they can do now is hope that their investments come back to even.)

If you followed the lessons presented in this book, you've already exited the market. You may have taken some losses (change that to, you *did* take some losses), but if you can get out of a bear market with less than 10 percent in losses, you're using a successful strategy. By the time the market stops falling, 10 percent losses will seem like a gift.

Do you remember when the bull market ended and it had one final parabolic climax? The same thing happens in a bear market, but in the opposite direction. As the bear market comes to an end, instead of a climax, there is a death spiral. When it's over, you have a market bottom.

Market Mastery

If you decide to buy on the dip (although it's a risky strategy and I'd advise against it), be sure to have strict stop losses in place so that if you're wrong, you can get out without pain. Remember the old rule "Don't try to catch a falling knife." Better yet, don't buy when the market is falling.

At the Bottom of the Market

Eventually, there are fewer and fewer sellers. Guess who steps into the market now? If you said buyers, you are right.

As the sellers slowly disappear, the buyers come in looking for bargains, which establishes a base for the next rally. One day, the bear market really ends, and the financial pain is reduced. All of the panicked sellers stop selling, and a bottom is created. This bottoming process can take a long while.

Those who lost money during the bear market are counting their losses, and deciding what to do next. More than likely, the market will go sideways for a lengthy time period before turning into another bull market.

There are usually clues that a bear market is on its last legs. Once again, you have to be alert to these clues, because you want to enter a bull market early and ride it as long as you can. Doing that can be a tremendously profitable experience.

Here are a few clues that a bear market is ending.

Financial Writers and Retail Investors Are Extremely Bearish

When you look at the American Association of Individual Investors (AAII) and Investors Intelligence sentiment readings, and the bearish sentiment is higher than 65 or 70 percent, that is a clue that the level of bearishness has become so high that no one in her right mind would invest in the market. Guess what? Because this is a contrarian indicator, it signals that it is (or will soon be) time to consider entering the market again. Still, you must be cautious not to enter too soon. Nevertheless, if too many people are bearish, and the market reaches extreme negative levels (such as 80 or 85 percent), that eventually provides a buying opportunity. To paraphrase a popular saying, when there is blood in the street, that is the time to buy.

These sentiment indicators have been quite accurate in the past, as long as they are not used to time the market. After all, people can remain pessimistic and negative about the stock market for a long time, even as the market is turning upward.

Even at the bottom, some fearful financial writers will make outlandishly extreme predictions, such as that the Dow will fall thousands of points lower (many said the opposite when the market was at a top). Just as you had to ignore the so-called experts when the market was at an all-time high, pay no attention to them when the market is at a multi-year low. Instead, concentrate on facts and figures.

Bottom Line

Don't forget that when the crowd is afraid, astute investors will look for an entry point.

Retail Investors Are Pouring Out of Equity Mutual Funds

Usually, the crowd is late in getting out of the market. As scared investors sell their stocks and equity mutual funds in a panic, that is a green light. In fact, one clue that the market may turn up again is that everyone hates the stock market, refuses to look at their 401(k)s, and doesn't want to talk about the market anymore.

As many investors sell all their stocks and the market falls rapidly, astute investors (who are interpreting clues) are looking for bargains. Never forget that retail investors have an established pattern of selling all their stocks near the bottom.

Market Mastery

It takes courage to step into the market while everyone else is fleeing, but it also could be one of the smartest financial moves you'll ever make. Nevertheless, until you become experienced, you should wait for a bullish signal to enter the market again rather than attempting to find the bottom.

These are clues that the market has bottomed, but you still need more hard evidence that the market is recovering before stepping in too quickly. If the bear market came after a crash, you must be on guard for a failed rally. Sometimes the smartest action to take is to sit on the sidelines and wait.

Good Economic News Is Ignored

You may find that a number of companies are reporting good earnings and beating low expectations. Because the mood of investors is so negative, though, the market ignores this good news. Like a boxer who got hit one too many times, investors are afraid to get back into the ring.

Of course, if economic conditions are really dreadful, you may have to wait years for a full recovery. Hopefully, something on the level of the 1929 downturn won't happen again, but if it does, the Fed will step in with its financial tools to improve the economy. The government will also do everything in its power to improve economic conditions.

Even as Wall Street tries to tell everyone to come back to the market again, investors won't believe it. After a bear market or crash, investors who have lost money are dismayed, shocked, and angry, and they will blame Wall Street.

End-of-Day Rallies on High Volume

Another clue that a new bull market may be forming is when rallies, which failed during the bear market, are successful. As you'll see when you look at the following indicators, you will find significant buy signals. Don't forget that the market goes up more than it goes down, so be prepared for the next rally, and don't make the mistake of being too negative when the rally begins.

For example, if the rallies are occurring on rising volume, this means that large institutions have stepped back into the market loaded with new buy orders. On a chart, you will see a series of higher highs and higher lows, which means buyers have entered the market and are moving the market higher. You must be patient, as this bullish scenario can take place over many weeks or months.

If the market starts the day by selling off but turns around and finishes higher on high volume, that is a significant bullish signal. It's particularly important if this turnaround happens at the end of the day. If there is a strong rally, it could carry over into the next day.

A lot depends on momentum. If there is strong volume, and momentum is to the upside, this is an extremely significant sign that the market is turning around. While others won't believe the market is coming back, you are already scaling in.

Bottom Line

Pay attention to rallies that occur on strong volume.

Market Mastery

If there is a quick selloff, analyze volume. If there is a selloff on low volume, however, this is a bullish sign. Even though the market is going down, there probably isn't enough institutional participation to bring the market much lower. Again, these aren't hard and fast rules, and there are exceptions, but you should watch volume closely.

When Market Indicators Say Buy

Here are the same market indicators I discussed earlier. When any of the indicators turn positive, it is bullish:

1. Moving Averages: Briefly, if the S&P 500 or other major indexes rise and stay above their 50-day, 100-day, or 200-day moving averages, this is a bullish signal. As you know, there are no guarantees, because no indicator is perfect, but it is an important clue. In fact, if the S&P 500 rises above its 200-day moving average, that is a significant signal to many investors that the market is making a strong comeback. Even if you don't pay attention to other indicators, pay attention to the mighty 200-day moving average.

2. MACD: When MACD crosses above its 9-day signal line or moves above the zero line (and stays above it), this is a bullish signal. Nevertheless, always confirm with other indicators and your own analysis before buying or selling. As you know, no signal is 100 percent reliable.

3. RSI: RSI tells you whether the market index is overbought or oversold. If RSI falls below 30, that is a signal that the market is in oversold territory. (Similarly, when RSI rises above 70, that signals an overbought market.) Unfortunately, RSI can remain overbought or oversold for long time periods before the index reverses direction. Nevertheless, it's useful in pointing out when the market is getting a bit extreme.

4. Chart Patterns: If the bear market is really coming to an end, when you look at a chart you might see patterns such as a double bottom. That occurs when the market does not break below major support levels and then reverses direction (twice). The second time it holds support, it forms what looks like a "W," which propels the market higher.

To summarize, market indicators are powerful tools, but they are only tools. They do not provide secrets, and are only a method to help determine which way the financial winds are blowing. Every brokerage firm, as well as major financial websites (listed in Chapter 14), will have charts and indicators. Again, use indicators in conjunction with your own observation and analysis.

Now that you have an idea of how a bear market begins and ends, in the next chapter let's look at strategies you can use during a bear market.

CHAPTER 10

Bear Market Strategies

If you are not prepared for a bear market and aren't sure what to do, this chapter will provide you with ideas.

Don't Be Scared—Be Prepared

If you are reading this chapter during a bear market, or believe one is coming, there is no reason to panic. If you collected the clues and deciphered them correctly, you should be able to get out of your positions early enough to avoid serious financial damage. Congratulations if you can accomplish that. Even if you are stuck in a bear market right now and have endured severe losses (over 50 percent), there's both good news and bad news.

The good news is that you have already lost so much that additional losses will probably be manageable. Most bear markets are short, lasting less than a year, and the end may already be near.

The bad news is that you lost a ton of money, so I'm sorry that this book did not find you sooner. However, since every bear market is different, be prepared for any outcome.

Make Money in a Bear Market

Many people fear bear markets because they cause so much financial and psychological damage. Nevertheless, during a downturn, there are strategies you can use to take advantage of it. Instead of being scared, you can profit.

If you can identify a bear market in its early stages, you can make money, and sometimes a lot of money. In fact, some astute traders do best during chaotic times, when the market is on the way down and large numbers of players are panicking. Although the vast majority of people hate corrections or bear markets, if you are willing to own bearish positions, you can prosper.

Once you have confirmed that a bear market has begun, you have two choices: You can flee (exit) or you can fight (own bearish positions). This chapter will examine both strategies, and you can decide which is more comfortable for you and your financial goals.

1. *Flee:* You make no attempt to profit from a falling market. Your goal is to exit long positions, protect your assets, and wait for an appropriate time to reinvest.
2. *Fight:* You hold positions that prosper when the market declines (such as selling short or holding inverse ETFs, which will be discussed next). Profiting from a falling market is simply another investment strategy that every investor should learn.

Fleeing from a Bear Market

Fleeing from a bear market is an easy strategy. You simply sell your stocks and move to cash. As long as you aren't selling in the later stages of a bear market, moving to the sidelines is a wise choice. Cash may not provide substantial returns; however, your goal is not to earn profits, but to avoid danger. Do not ignore tax consequences, but avoiding losses is more important than worrying about how much you pay in taxes (talk to a tax professional, though, before taking any action).

Fighting with a Bear Market

Instead of running away from an approaching bear market and hiding in cash, you can profit from the downturn. There are a number of strategies you can adopt. Here are a few ideas, although the strategy you choose depends on your risk tolerance and financial goals, as well as your comfort level.

Strategy #1: Buy and Hold

The first strategy is the simplest: Hold long positions through the bear market and wait until it's over. Doing nothing is always the easiest strategy and requires no thought and no action. You already know that many of the most successful investors recommend you stay the course through a bear market. That's good advice for readers who lack the confidence to study the clues and act on the signals.

If you're a long-term investor and you can withstand market volatility, consider staying the course. Although it's best to exit a bear market early, this isn't easy to accomplish. Therefore, for the many investors who don't have the skill (or desire) to time their entry and exit, buy-and-hold is a reasonable investment approach.

Unfortunately, buy-and-hold can also be the most emotionally difficult. It's hard because as the market falls, you are losing money every day when your once profitable stocks and indexes turn into losses, and it's tempting to sell. As you know, most retail investors sell at the very bottom, just when the bear market is about to end.

The good news is that eventually painful bear markets turn around—often sooner than later—and many of your losing stocks will recover along with the market indexes.

Nevertheless, if you do see a bear market approaching, although you don't have to sell your entire portfolio, it's a good idea to move some money to cash. In other words, increase the cash portion of your portfolio while reducing the equity portion.

Bottom Line

You must decide whether adopting the buy-and-hold strategy works for you. Usually the biggest obstacle to surviving a bear market is your emotions, especially fear. If this strategy is to work, you must be willing to withstand financial pain. If you are going to buy and hold, I recommend doing it with market indexes rather than individual stocks. During a bear market, many individual stocks get slaughtered, and some never recover.

Strategy #2: Cut Your Losses (or Lock in Gains)

Your ultimate goal is to exit all positions before a bear market can inflict serious losses. If the bear market is just beginning (you may not know for a while), you still have time to cut your losses and get out.

Assuming you've followed the advice given in this book, you have been collecting clues and observing the overall condition of the market. If you are not convinced that a bear market has arrived but believe that one is looming, then slowly scale out of your holdings. How much to sell depends on the confidence you have in your analysis.

For example, if you own index funds, and you are not ready to exit 100 percent, you can sell 25 to 30 percent of your portfolio. Based on your analysis and indicators, you can continue to scale out depending on the evolving condition of the market. Once you are convinced that the bear market is real (based on facts, not opinion), then sell 100 percent. Stop selling anytime your analysis is incorrect or if you were too early.

If you own individual stocks and have losses of 7 to 8 percent, it's recommended that you cut your losses and sell (although you should determine your own target prices). Hoping that your stocks will come back to former levels is not a strategy but a wish. On the other hand, if you have a chance to escape a bear market with only 5 to 7 percent losses, by all means do so. Finally, if you own stocks that have questionable prospects for the future, cut your losses and sell without looking back.

As you know from reading this book, you are not trying to time the market each week or day (that is for short-term traders). Instead, you are looking for major signals.

Unfortunately, sometimes the signals aren't clear; often, you'll get conflicting information. In that case, you can wait until everything lines up perfectly (rarely does that happen), or you can make a decision to scale out of the market, that is, to reduce your position.

Much later you'll know which was the right decision, but to avoid losing money in a bear market, eventually you must make an exit decision. Your decision about when to do so will depend on your risk tolerance.

Bottom Line

If you're not sure what to do, reduce position size and cut your losses. One of the biggest mistakes that people make is holding on to losing stocks. It's true that some stocks may come back to even one day, but that is not a chance you want to take. Once you have definitively identified a bear market, get out, and stay out—the sooner the better.

Market Mastery

If you have received signals from market indicators and clues and decide to sell part of your portfolio, sell stocks that have lost money.

Strategy #3: Move to Cash

If a bear market is vicious, you should consider selling some or all of your stocks. By safely hiding out in cash, you can avoid losing money. One advantage of cash is that it's liquid, which means you can enter and exit very quickly. Of course, you can consider alternative investments such as gold or bonds, but cash is the easiest choice.

Although you may not make much money if you're in cash during a bear market, at least you're not losing any. That is why cash is a reasonable strategy. In fact, for the sake of diversification, it always makes sense to have some cash on the sidelines for emergencies.

The Disadvantages of Holding Cash

The biggest problem with cash is that you can lose money to inflation over the long term (especially in low-interest-rate environments). However, you must ignore such thoughts when your purpose is to exit a dangerous market.

In a sideways or bear market, moving to cash for protection makes sense, but you don't want to stay there too long. Some people are so afraid of a bear market that they refuse to re-enter the stock market, even when a new bull market begins. And if you stay out of the market permanently because you're afraid, you've lost the opportunity to build wealth. Therefore, if you decide to move to cash, evaluate whether this is an unemotional decision or whether you are under duress. Do not liquidate your investments out of fear.

As long as you don't permanently put most of your money in a low-paying money market account or CD, being in cash may be necessary—at least until you find another investment. Nevertheless, there have been times when interest rates have spiked, so the returns on CDs and money market accounts have been excellent. If a money market account or CD is paying more than 4 or 5 percent, owning these investments might not be such a bad idea.

Bottom Line

As soon as the clues and analysis tell you that the bear market is over, begin scaling back into the market. Eventually you will put that cash to work during the next bull market—assuming you analyzed the clues correctly.

Strategy #4: Buy and Hold Inverse ETFs (but Not Forever)

If you want to capitalize on an upcoming market pullback or correction, consider investing in *nonleveraged* inverse ETFs. Because few people have the discipline to manage short positions, it's better to buy inverse ETFs rather than to sell individual stocks short. Essentially, an inverse ETF tracks or mimics the *inverse* of a specific index. Therefore, if a major market index goes down (which it tends to do in a bear market), the inverse ETF rises. Inverse ETFs are easy to manage and are less risky compared with selling stocks short.

Buying an inverse ETF means you are going long an index fund that earns profits when the market declines.

Here's an example of how they work. The inverse ETF for the S&P 500 is SH (NYSE:SH). Therefore, if the S&P 500 declines, SH gains value. This ETF inversely imitates the performance of the S&P 500 on a 1 to 1 basis. If the S&P 500 goes down by 2 percent, then SH goes up by 2 percent. Conversely, if the S&P 500 goes *up* by 3 percent, then SH will go *down* by 3 percent.

The following are four of the most popular nonleveraged inverse ETFs, investments that should potentially make money during bear markets:

1. SH: This ETF is an inverse of the S&P 500. When the S&P goes down, SH goes up.
2. DOG: This ETF is an inverse of the Dow Jones Industrial Average (DJIA). When the Dow goes down, DOG goes up.

3. PSQ: This ETF is an inverse of the Nasdaq-100. When the Nasdaq-100 goes down, PSQ goes up.
4. RWM: This ETF is an inverse of the Russell 2000. When the Russell 2000 goes down, RWM goes up.

Nonleveraged inverse ETFs such as these are ideal for aggressive traders or investors who want to own bearish positions during a bear market rather than wait on the sidelines.

Bottom Line

For those who want to profit in a bear market, cash is not really king. It is a high-ranking official. On the other hand, buying inverse funds (or selling stocks short) during a bear market is the real king.

Avoid Leveraged ETFs

Avoid buying *leveraged* inverse ETF funds unless you are a day trader. The reasons are a bit complex (one reason is that leveraged ETFs must be rebalanced each day, so trading expenses add up), but the end result is the same: It is a mistake to hold leveraged ETFs overnight.

Also be careful when buying bear market mutual funds that short the market because these specialized funds impose sales loads and redemption fees on customers who exit before owning the shares for at least thirty or sixty days. You're better off buying an inverse ETF if you want to own bearish investments because there are no additional fees.

Bottom Line

Although buying inverse ETFs is an ideal strategy in a bear market, stay away from the leveraged kind. The only time leveraged ETFs make sense is if you are day trading or using other short-term trading tactics.

Managing Inverse ETFs

As with any other investment, if you do buy inverse ETFs, you must use strict risk-management tactics. Almost everyone wants the market to go up, so by betting against the market you are betting against Wall Street, as well as the millions of people who are invested in 401(k)s and IRAs. It's not just Wall Street that wants bullish markets. The sitting president also has an interest in seeing the market rise, and the Fed has used tactics to keep the market from plunging too much.

Although betting against the market is a legitimate strategy, your bearish views on the market will be as welcome as a skunk at a garden party. This does not mean you should not buy inverse ETFs, but it's a challenging strategy. Since the whole world wants the market to go up, betting against the market takes patience and fortitude, even more so than going long. Still, a bear market is a fact of life, so there is no reason why you shouldn't make a profit from it.

Only consider buying inverse ETFs, however, in a bearish environment. If you make the mistake of buying inverse funds because the market has hit an all-time high, betting against the market could be a money-losing mistake. Remember that the market can go much higher than what seems logical.

If you do buy inverse funds (or sell stocks short), and you are losing more than 5 percent, consider scaling out of your position. If losses are as high as 7 or 8 percent, sell. It means your timing was wrong. You can buy back the inverse ETFs and reestablish the position when conditions are right (i.e., the market is falling). If you follow this rule, you will save yourself a small fortune over time.

Most important for your sanity and investment portfolio: Don't become a permabear, someone who is always negative on the stock market. It's almost as bad as being a permabull, who believes in the bull market so much that he can't imagine a significant decline.

Being a permabear or a permabull will cost you money.

Strategy #5: Sell on the Rallies (or Add to Your Inverse Funds)

As you know, during a bull market, some investors use a risky strategy called "buying on the dip." During a bear market, however, you can do the opposite, that is, buy more shares of the inverse ETF if there is a bear market rally. This is a risky strategy, though—it's just as risky to sell on the rally as to buy on the dip.

It's very easy to get the timing wrong. For example, there may be a short-term rally in the middle of a bear market, which you assume will fail. With that assumption, you buy more shares of an inverse ETF, but instead of failing the market goes much, much higher (though, since it's a bear market, the rally will eventually fail). These bear market rallies can be very strong. Unless you are an experienced short-term trader, this strategy is not recommended, but at least you know how it works.

Strategy #6: Use Shorting Strategies

Instead of buying inverse ETFs, in a bear market you can also sell individual stocks short. Briefly, instead of buying low and selling high, you do the opposite: You sell a stock that you don't own (your brokerage firm will lend you the shares), and plan to buy it back at a lower price when it falls. In other words, sell high and cover the position lower.

Most investors learn early in their investing careers that shorting stocks is a very risky—and therefore inadvisable—investment strategy. Despite the fact that this is conventional wisdom, it makes little sense. When we own stock, we lose a lot of money when the price declines. Yet no one tells investors that owning stock is anything but a prudent investment strategy. Guess what? Shorting is just the opposite strategy. Yes, you can lose money if the stock rallies. And yes, you can lose a huge amount (in theory there is no upper limit to a stock price) if you don't manage your risk.

Nevertheless, shorting is just the opposite of buying and is a well-recognized investment technique.

Keep in mind that shorting is not for every trader. If this strategy makes you uncomfortable (despite the previous explanation), then your investing strategy will be to earn money during bull markets and to sit on the sidelines during bear markets. If you're an experienced short seller who knows how to manage risk, then by all means, sell stocks short at the appropriate time. Most investors, however, can attempt to profit during a bear market by buying inverse ETFs. Understanding and using inverse ETFs is easier than attempting to find specific stocks to short.

Bottom Line

Selling short is for experienced traders who use stop losses and other strict money management tactics to avoid losing money. Although, like all strategies, it carries some amount of risk, it's a perfectly legitimate market strategy.

Strategy #7: Speculate with Put Options

Another way to profit during a bear market is to speculate by buying put options. Buying a *put* option usually refers to taking a short position in a stock (because you believe the stock will fall in value). In other words, if you believe that the underlying stock price will go down (or fear it will and want to protect your investment), you can buy a put. Therefore, if the underlying stock goes down in price, the put option usually goes up. One huge advantage of buying a put option is that it's less risky than shorting stock. Unfortunately, most speculators lose money with options, primarily because they don't truly understand how options work. Hint: Don't jump into options without first learning more about them.

After a Bear Market, When Should You Get Back In?

Let's say that you correctly predicted an approaching bear market and that you decided to move some of your holdings to cash. Perhaps you bought inverse ETFs and made a profit as the market went lower. Now what?

When your analysis tells you that the bear has gone into hibernation, you will have to decide when it is safe to go long again and reinvest. Obviously, if you held your index ETFs or index funds through the bear market, you do not have to worry about market timing. You're already in. On the other hand, if you got out in time, you can re-enter. It takes courage to buy when others are afraid. In fact, very few people enter the market at the lows, and that's fine. It's nearly impossible to know until after the fact the precise moment when the market has made its low. The important thing is to be able to observe market trends and to know when they are long term and not temporary fluctuations.

At this point, the investing crowd is shell-shocked and is probably afraid to invest. Those who lost money on the way down are scared of an even worse crash. In their minds, the financial world has come to an end. Investors are so afraid they stay permanently in bonds, money market accounts, CDs, or a savings account.

After a lengthy bear market, which could be paired with a nasty recession, few investors are willing to take a chance on the stock market. As for you, this is the time to keep your head and do the opposite of everyone else. Look for other opportunities to go long, based on actual evidence rather than emotion. Eventually, the stock market and the country recover. Although there are those who are still in disbelief, the market slowly comes back from the doldrums and a bull market starts anew.

Been Down So Long Looks Like Up to Me

Although it's easy to spend a lot of time and energy being angry about how much money you lost in a bear market, there's another choice. Ignore the lost money and focus on current opportunities. Thousands of stocks are now at bargain prices. Don't forget that the stock market is an auction, and you want to get competitive prices for each of your transactions. If the market is having a half-off sale, by all means participate as the market climbs out of the doldrums. Just be sure to use strict money management tactics to avoid entering too early (and pay attention to the clues and indicators).

To paraphrase Warren Buffett, sell when others are greedy and buy when others are fearful. When fear is high and no one wants to buy stocks, this might be the time to begin scaling back into the market.

When to Get Back Into the Market Again

If you sold all your stocks because you were afraid of losing all your money, you might be afraid to go long again. That would be a mistake, given that the market has a long-term upward bias. Because of fear, you might be giving up some very profitable future financial opportunities.

To avoid sitting indefinitely on the sidelines, consult market indicators. As mentioned before, one of the easiest indicators to use and interpret is moving averages. As you recall, when the indexes are above their 100-day or 200-day moving averages, that is a bullish sign. Because this is a lagging indicator, however, you cannot wait too long to confirm the buying opportunity.

In addition, take a look at MACD to see if it's pointing up. Finally, you can use sentiment indicators such as VIX, and surveys such as the AAII and Investors Intelligence. Sentiment indicators give you a clue as to what retail investors are thinking. The more bearish and fearful they are, the more bullish things look for the market.

It is reasonable to believe that "now is always the most difficult time to invest." However, just because it may be difficult does not suggest that you should hide and be afraid of making decisions.

Bottom Line

When there are storm clouds above and it appears as if the market will never recover, re-entering is not easy. However, you must look for new financial opportunities. This is a time when you need courage. As long as you don't enter too soon, and scale in slowly, you will be able to make money. Remember this: The most profitable period of a bull market is the first year or two, so be ready to participate.

Now that you know how to manage a bear market, let's look at two attributes of successful investors: patience and fortitude.

CHAPTER 11

Patience and Fortitude

If you visit the New York City Public Library, you'll see two lions in front of the building on either side of the main entrance on Fifth Avenue. They are named Patience and Fortitude. To be a successful investor or trader, you need to have the characteristics of these two lions.

It takes patience to hold a position for months or years even though the crowds are warning that you are wrong. You also need patience to give your strategies time to work. Along the way, it's easy to get distracted by financial commentators who are perpetually bullish or by those who are perpetually bearish. Focusing on the facts is not easy when people are bombarding you with conflicting information.

It also takes fortitude to enter the market when others are fleeing, or to flee the market while others are entering. Doing the opposite of the crowds, and your own instincts, takes courage.

And Then There's Prudence

If I could, I would add a third lion to the duo of Patience and Fortitude. Her name is Prudence (which makes her a lioness). While it is wonderful to have the courage of your convictions and the patience to wait for them to come true, you must always be a prudent investor. Therefore, while planning for the best outcome, you are also prepared for the worst. Anticipating worst-case scenarios is the reason you buy ETFs that track the major indexes, the reason you use stop losses, the reason you diversify, the reason you occasionally protect your portfolio with put options, the reason you do not follow the crowd for too long, and the reason you try to balance the twin emotions of fear and greed.

Being prudent also means assessing market conditions so that you are not caught off guard when there is a bear market. It means taking some money off the table on occasion and locking in profits. This is a nice way of saying "Don't be greedy." Unfortunately, in the heat of the market battle, it's not always easy to know when you are taking advantage of a profitable opportunity and when you're simply motivated by greed.

Sitting Tight Makes the Big Money

The hardest thing for most people to do in the stock market is nothing. We always feel as if we must do something, but far too often that's the wrong move. For example, sitting and waiting during a bull market without making a trade is hard for some people, even if their investments are unprofitable.

In *Reminiscences of a Stock Operator*, Livermore made another discovery:

> *"After spending many years on Wall Street and after making and losing millions of dollars, I want to tell you this: It was never my thinking that made the big money for me. It always was my sitting. Got that? My sitting tight! It is no trick at all to be right on the market. You always find lots of early bulls in bull markets and early bears in bear markets. I've know many [traders] who were right at exactly the right time, and began buying and selling stocks when prices were at the very level which would show the greatest profit. And their experience invariably matched mine— that is, they made no real money out of it. [Traders] who can*

be both right and sit tight are uncommon. I found it one of the hardest things to learn. But it is only after a stock operator has firmly grasped this that he can make big money."

Be Disciplined but Also Flexible

Many people know that they must be disciplined if they want to be a successful investor or trader. This sounds easy . . . that is, until the markets are plunging, your diversification formulas aren't working, and you're scared of losing everything. During extreme conditions, most investors discover they aren't disciplined.

In addition to being disciplined, you must also be flexible. Not every market is the same, nor is every financial situation. Although creating a plan and sticking to it are essential, there are times when you have to act fast to avoid losing money. That is when you need flexibility.

It's a rare investor who possesses both qualities. It means knowing when to sit and wait for your plan to work and also when to put on the brakes and cut losses.

Another common mistake is sticking with a losing position because you're certain that the market is wrong. If you insist on being proven right and won't cut your losses, there is only one winner: the market. Please leave your ego behind before you invest in the market.

In reality, it's hard to manage money, especially your own money. As you already know, the simplest solution is to buy and hold, and not worry about it. For decades, this strategy worked as the market generally climbed higher. Unfortunately, there are also long periods when buy-and-hold doesn't work, and after several years, you may end up about where you started.

Finally, being flexible means that you will not lock yourself into a permabull or permabear mentality. Once you have lost your objectivity and flexibility, you might as well let someone else manage your money.

Bottom Line

Be flexible enough to switch positions and strategies if the evidence proves you wrong.

Market Mastery

It's so simple to say "Don't get emotional about money." But experience tells us that when the market is at extreme levels and moving quickly, keeping your emotions under control is challenging. All of us have stories of how our emotions caused us to lose money; here's mine.

Several years ago, I had prepared for a positive Fed announcement by increasing my long position with ETFs that mimic the broad-based indexes, as well as a few individual stocks. Fifteen minutes before the announcement, an acquaintance of mine who worked in a large New York bond firm called me with urgent news.

"Sell everything!" he yelled. "The Fed is not going to cut interest rates. The market is going to crash!" Then he slammed down the phone.

I got the feeling he knew something that I didn't know. I also had no reason to believe that his information was inaccurate. After all, he worked on Wall Street. Instead of sticking with my plan, or scaling back a little because of the warning, I panicked. I sold three-fourths of my position for small gains. If my well-connected bond acquaintance was right, my puny profits would have turned into losses in fifteen minutes.

At 2:00 P.M. ET, the Fed announced that they were cutting interest rates. Big surprise! The market rallied by more than 2 percent, and I lost out on one of the most profitable two-day gains in history. (Ironically, the market did crash six months later.)

Bottom Line

After you create an investment or trading plan, stick to it. Only change the plan if you have solid evidence (technical or fundamental) that something has changed. Don't get sidetracked by the opinions of well-meaning but emotional acquaintances or friends, or by a stranger on TV.

If you believe in yourself and the strategies you are using, you won't get talked out of a position, or change your mind because you just read a convincing article on why you should sell all your stocks now.

One well-known columnist spent four years warning about an imminent stock market crash. Instead of crashing, however, the market went up over 30 percent. Anyone who followed his advice missed out on huge profits. People who continually warn of market crashes have an ailment I call "Crashitis." One day they'll be right, of course, but meanwhile they're missing out on years of potential gains.

Unless there is evidence that the market is going to reverse or appears to be in a bubble, stick with the trend. Once you make the market your friend, you have the most powerful ally in the world: underlying market conditions.

Don't Add to Losing Positions

It's happened dozens of times. Investors are sure the market has gone up too far and too fast, and they start betting against it. Unless you have solid evidence and not just a feeling or opinion, exercise prudence and move to the sidelines. If the market is moving higher, the odds are good it will continue in that direction. The same thing applies to a market that's moving downward.

But what do you do if you *know* the market trend is about to change? Let's think this through. Based on your study of underlying market conditions as revealed by key indicators, you know you are right: The market cannot go higher (or lower) much longer. So you make your bet—and it is a bet, not an investment. There's a risk, of course: If you're too early, you've lost money. The key is flexibility. If you see that the market, contrary to your expectations, is moving in the wrong direction, you must be willing to reevaluate your position. Many investors, because they are sure they are right, will not cut their losses and wait for another opportunity. Instead, they add more to a losing position. It's worth repeating: Don't add money to a losing position (with few exceptions).

If you are certain you are right about the market's direction, why not test your bullish or bearish view with a small position of, say, no more than 5 percent? If you are right, in no time you will see green on your screen. Then, by all means, start adding to that winning position.

If you're wrong, hold the small position as a way of monitoring the market and as a reminder of how much money you could have lost if you had bet everything. (If that small position gets uncomfortable, unload it and take the small loss.)

Let's say that after several months, the market really reverses. Guess what? Your losing 5 percent position begins to turn green again. That is the time to start scaling into the position.

Bottom Line

When there are selloffs and rallies, you don't want to be first, but you don't want to be last, either. It's okay to give up that first 5 or 7 percent of any move, but after that, you should have more than enough evidence to begin to follow the trend.

Don't Be Too Late

Not quite as dangerous to your wealth is being too late to a bull or bear market. Here's what often happens: There has been a bear market and people are so negative they refuse to invest. Meanwhile, the market grinds higher and higher.

After several years of gains, the media suddenly writes stories of how the market is back where it started or is at all-time highs. At that point, people who were afraid to invest decide to buy stocks. In fact, there is panic buying, and people can't buy stocks, ETFs, and stock mutual funds fast enough.

You know how this story ends. The bull market continues to go higher for a few more months, or maybe a year, and just as clueless investors bet their life savings on the market, the rally stops and reverses direction.

When you see "everyone" wanting to buy stocks, this is a clue that you should start scaling out of your positions. After all, when the market starts to crack, you must get out and stay out.

Market Mastery

Remember that you can find out what the crowd is doing by monitoring the AAII and Investors Intelligence sentiment surveys, by paying attention to mutual fund purchases, and checking current margin levels. When any indicator gets to extreme levels, the media will report that "inflows into stock mutual funds have reached all-time highs." Guess what? That's another clue!

Don't Bring Your Anger and Biases to the Market

Someone who is angry about the economy, the world, the stock market, or the government is not going to make wise investments. If you allow your politics or biases about the world and economy to influence your investing decisions, it will be hard to succeed in the market. Your love or hate of political parties or the president can get in the way of making an objective assessment of market conditions. Anger and rage, as well as other emotions, are harmful to market participants.

If you're friends with overly opinionated investors, don't take investment advice from them. If they're yelling at you to buy a certain stock, think about doing the opposite of what they say (a strategy that may work because going against the crowd is often the right move). Once you've lost the ability to recognize reality, then every decision you make will be influenced by biases, fears, and prejudices. More than likely, it will cost you.

Don't Get Angry at the Market

If you manage your own money and make mistakes, don't blame the market. The market is not a perfect system and is not always fair to individual investors. However, even with all its faults it's still one of the best places to build wealth.

If you aren't prepared with the right tools, attitude, and knowledge, it's hard to win the stock market game. Although it may satisfy your ego to blame the "unfair market" for any losses, it's not worth your time or energy. The market is what it is: a gigantic mass of buyers and sellers with different emotions and goals.

Bottom Line

Getting too emotional about the market is a ticket to disaster. If you let your bullish or bearish bias (without appropriate signals to justify that bias) influence your investment decisions, it will be difficult to make money. It doesn't matter what you "think" should happen to the market. The only thing that matters is what the market thinks. Therefore, the only emotion you should have about the stock market is neutrality. Here's a hint: If you make the market your friend, perhaps it will lead you in the right direction.

The Pretend Reason of the Day

One of the most amusing games played by the media is explaining (i.e., guessing) why the market goes up or down every day. They offer many reasons, some of which have nothing to do with reality. Even more entertaining, different news sources give different— often opposing—reasons for the market's rise or fall.

If the Dow declined yesterday, one news source might say it's because the market didn't like an earnings report from a particular company. Another source might pinpoint a rumor that the Fed was going to raise or lower interest rates. Still others might report that it happened because the dollar fell or there was an uprising in a remote village in Mexico.

The funniest part is that financial commentators want you to believe the market is logical. In fact, the more you become involved with the market, the more you realize that in the short term its rises and falls are profoundly irrational.

As I said before, it would be more useful if you knew what is happening (or may in the future) rather than *why* it happened. For example, if the Fed is having a meeting and may lower or raise interest rates, then you can expect the market to react. That is a market-moving event (especially if the decision is a surprise). The question is not why this change is occurring but how the market will react.

Because it's usually too late for you to know the reason the market went up or down each day, the best you can do is watch for clues. For now, remember that the reason that's given each day often has little to do with reality (with few exceptions).

"They" Are Making the Market Move

Some beginners (and a few experienced ones who lost money) may tell you that the markets are manipulated by a mysterious group of people: "They." For example, some short sellers will claim that "they" wanted the market to go up today, which is why there was a rally.

These investors believe that the mysterious "they" force institutions to buy or sell each day, and the little guys like you and me aren't privy to the secret instructions. Other people believe there is a Wizard of Wall Street secretly pulling levers to make the market rise or fall. Even more people believe that there is a secret government group, the Plunge Protection Team (PPT), created to keep the market from falling. The rumor of the PPT began after the 1987 crash. In reality, the group is the Working Group on Financial Markets and was created in 1988 to make recommendations to various government groups such as the Fed to prevent economic turmoil. (After a number of market crashes, few people mention the PPT, but this myth is likely to return in the future.)

And Yet . . . Buyer Beware

Although the idea of a market cabal sounds a bit paranoid, unfortunately, some of what these investors say has been true in the past. Throughout the market's history, powerful people have attempted to manipulate the markets through the media, or by creating unregulated large investment pools (one of the reasons for the 1929 crash) that move the markets in one direction or another.

In an infamous case, Herbert and Nelson Hunt, billionaire brothers from Texas, tried to manipulate the price of silver in 1973. The Hunts began to accumulate large quantities of silver (200 million ounces, to be exact), and leveraged their holdings many times over. The price of silver went from $1.95 an ounce to more than $48.50 an ounce in 1979, forming a gigantic silver bubble.

With assistance from the Fed, the Commodities Exchange (COMEX) changed the rules regarding leverage, and prevented the Hunt brothers, or anyone else, from manipulating silver. The government did everything in its power to deflate the price of silver, and its price began to fall.

Capitulation occurred on March 27, 1980, when silver fell by more than 50 percent (from $21.62 to $10.80). As a result of the silver crash, the Hunt brothers were no longer billionaires (Nelson Bunker Hunt filed for bankruptcy), and they had to pay huge fines to the IRS; in addition, Nelson Hunt was banned from trading in the commodities market.

There are other ways that people try to influence individual stocks. For example, in the past, stock analysts had the power to move stocks up or down by changing their buy or sell ratings. Therefore, if an analyst rated XYZ as a buy, the stock might go up by 5 or 10 percent. Although this power has gradually lessened after several bear markets, to protect yourself, you can ignore the hype (but be aware that it exists) and focus on the charts, indicators, and clues.

The lesson here is that when investing in the stock market, you should always be cautious. That means not investing in penny stocks, not investing in anything you don't understand, researching stocks before investing, and sticking with reputable, well-known brokerage firms.

Don't Fall in Love with Your Investments

You may love a company and its product, but if you are unable to view it objectively, you will lose money. For example, some very smart investors fell in love with gold for all the right reasons. Even though their logic was sound and gold went up to astronomical levels, they were convinced it would climb even higher. Even though they were gold experts, and had a dozen logical reasons why gold should go higher, in fact it went through a two-year correction. You may love any investment, but once it falls below its 50-day moving average, 100-day moving average, and then its 200-day moving average, it is time to sell. You can be completely logical but still lose money.

Here's another true story: One of my acquaintances noticed that the U.S. economy was getting weaker, that there was a slowdown in Asia, that debt in the United States was growing by huge amounts, and that there was turmoil in the Middle East. When he thought about the world's problems, he concluded that the U.S. stock market could not possibly go higher. So he started shorting the market.

Even with all the problems in the world, the market kept going up. My acquaintance, convinced he was right, kept adding to his short positions. After two years of shorting unsuccessfully and being too stubborn to cover his positions, he was finally ready to give up. He could not believe he could be so wrong; his losses exceeded 50 percent. Meanwhile, the market continued to rise.

His biggest mistake—and the mistake of all such investors—was thinking he was smarter than the market. He bet against it too early, and because he didn't use stop losses and was too stubborn to admit that he was wrong, he took a huge hit. When the market finally plunged, as he'd predicted it would do, he eventually made some of his money back—but not most of it.

Bottom Line

Don't fight with the market. When a favorite stock is performing poorly, and when market conditions are bearish, don't be afraid to get rid of it. You can always buy the stock again when market conditions are better (and the probability of making money has increased).

The Market Is Always Right

No matter what happens behind the scenes, the most important lesson is this: The market is always right. You may believe it's too high or too low and should surge or fall, but your opinion doesn't matter. In the end, the market always wins.

Many people incorrectly believe that to be successful in the market, you need to be smarter than other people. Although being smart is helpful, it does not guarantee success. In fact, some of the smartest people I've known lost tons of money in the market. Why? They believe the market is logical—or worse, they think they are smarter than the market. After all, the market is moved by the emotions of millions of market participants, especially institutions.

Often the market goes up even though there is bad news. In other words, perception (and anticipation of what might happen in the future) moves the market as much as the fundamentals such as a company's earnings or revenue.

Marc Faber, a well-known short seller, discussed his experiences when he was shorting the market near the end of 1999.

"I had heavily shorted high-tech stocks in 1998 and subsequently I lost a ton of money. This episode is really a dark spot in my life as an investor and investment advisor. It taught me several lessons that I shall never forget. What I think about markets is completely irrelevant. What matters is what other people think about them.

"Fundamentally, I was right about the coming collapse of the Nasdaq; however, for as long as the majority of other investors believed in the 'New Economy' theme, high-tech and communication stocks continued to appreciate."

Don't try to outsmart the market. You can be right and still lose money. Instead, rely on patience, fortitude, and prudence to see you through bad times and take advantage of good times.

In the next chapter, we'll look at the ways you can reduce stock market risk.

CHAPTER 12

How to Reduce Risk

If you are relatively new to the market, and even if you're not, this is an important chapter. After all, no matter how good your strategy, no matter how perfect your timing, if you don't manage risk, you will lose money, and sometimes a lot of money.

Recognize that if you are going to participate in the market, there will always be some risk. One of your goals while in the market is to reduce or limit that risk. If you want to eliminate all market risk, then buy Treasuries (although you can lose money to inflation). If you plan to be a long-term participant in the stock market, however, you must be willing to accept some risk.

When managing risk, you should have an idea of how much you are willing to lose on each investment. Although you don't expect to lose, you must prepare for losses in advance. After all, even with the best analysis, it's possible to be wrong. That is why it's so important not to get stubborn and refuse to cut losses. It's essential that when investing in the stock market you accept reality. As discussed earlier, never forget that the market has the final word. Never be so confident in your view of the market that you set yourself up for a gigantic loss.

There are two main ways to manage risk: You can use mechanical tools or you can change your behavior by keeping your emotions under control. Many people are influenced by opinions and emotions, and end up following their instincts, which are often misleading.

Finally, risk tolerance is a personal decision that is influenced by your financial goals and time horizon. Someone who is near retirement will likely have less risk tolerance than a college student, but not always. Most important, you must be comfortable with the amount of risk you take. For many investors, being diversified into different asset classes (e.g., bonds, stocks, fixed income) helps reduce risk. As you know, one of main advantages of buying market indexes is that it provides instant diversification.

Reduce Risk by Trading Indexes

As we've discussed throughout the book, one of the best ways to reduce risk is to buy ETFs that track the major indexes rather than buying individual stocks. Typically, major market indexes don't move up or down more than 1 percent each day (unless the market is especially volatile), while many stocks move that much and more every day. Because indexes are so diversified, it takes a huge market selloff or rally to move them to extreme levels.

Here's the tradeoff: You can make a lot more money with individual stocks. Like a mini-lottery ticket, over the short or long term the right stock can generate a small fortune. During rallies, it's wonderful to own those high-flying stocks. But when those rallies turn to selloffs, you'll be thankful that you are investing in market indexes.

Another reason why the risk averse should trade indexes: Although you can buy and hold indexes without worrying too much about the day-to-day fluctuations, with many individual stocks, you must monitor the position very closely.

If You Buy Stocks

Even though this book recommends owning indexes, many people like to own stocks. Therefore, most of the following advice pertains primarily to those who hold stocks or ETFs and not index funds. However, even if you are only holding indexes, this advice should also be useful.

How People Love Tips!

Shhh, don't tell anyone. What if I told you that I have a stock that will rise by 30 percent within a week? And you better buy it right now because it might be too late. Yes, people fall for this line every day, and sometimes not just beginners.

Some tipsters are the smartest people in the room, and they know a lot more about the stock market than you. (If you ask them, they'll tell you.) There is only one problem: They are almost always wrong.

It's not just acquaintances and friends who give tips. Every day, know-it-alls appear on TV touting the hottest stock of the day (by then, it's already gone up by over 20 percent). In addition, every week there are tons of articles on what stocks to buy. Here's a tip: If you have to get your stock ideas from someone on TV or from an acquaintance, you will lose money.

Bottom Line

Your ultimate goal is to find your own stock ideas (or better yet, choose index funds) so you don't have to listen to the tipsters.

Cutting Losses While Letting Winners Run (but Not Forever)

An important rule of investing is to cut losses so that you never lose more than a predetermined amount from any one trade. That accomplishes the major goal of risk management. Another worthwhile rule is to allow winners to run. In other words, when the market is moving in your direction, and you have a winning position, do not be tempted to sell for quick profits. Yes, you can scale back by selling a portion of your holdings at any time, but do not take profits too soon. Every trade doesn't work exactly as planned, but capitalizing on winning trades is one of your goals.

Similarly, when a trade is not working as expected, be ready to get out. This is mandatory. When the market tells you to be in cash, sell all your holdings. Do not be afraid to take small losses. Likewise, when you get a bullish signal, you want to be in on the long side (although not 100 percent of your assets).

The general guideline is this: If you own individual stocks or indexes and have losses of 7 or 8 percent, that is the time to sell. Sell losers before they turn into even bigger losers. Obviously, a lot depends on underlying market conditions.

If the selloff is in the middle of a strong bull market, there's a good probability that the market will recover, and soon. In that case, holding the index might be a prudent decision. However, if you own a poorly performing individual stock, give it up and find a better investment.

If the selloff appears at the beginning of a bear market, sell even earlier, perhaps when you have a 5 percent loss. If your market clues tell you the market trend is headed lower, then selling at this point is mandatory.

Conversely, if you have previous profits, let the winners run as long as feasible. At times, it makes sense to scale out of positions to lock in profits. Just remember that your overall approach is not to sell the entire position until the market clues confirm that the bull market is over. Taking profits on a portion of your position is part of prudent risk management. If you have too much money invested in one position (because of a substantial price increase), then it makes sense to sell a portion and either reallocate those funds to another bullish investment or allocate more of your portfolio to cash.

Selling is not an easy decision to make, unless you buy and never sell, which works for a while in certain market environments. There's a delicate balance between knowing when to put on the gas (add to your positions) and when to lighten up.

Don't Make Impulsive Investments

One sure way of losing money is making impulsive trades or investments. If you get an urge to make a trade immediately, similar to how a gambler feels before pulling the lever on a slot machine, stop and think. Take the time to analyze why you must make the trade now.

If you find that you can't help yourself and feel compelled to make that impulsive trade, you are crossing the line from investing to gambling. Once you do that, it's hard to turn back.

Bottom Line

Don't let emotions control investment decisions. One of the best ways to eliminate impulsive trades is to create a plan and write a list of rules. Then look at those rules before buying or selling a stock.

Use Tools to Reduce Risk

Since it is so difficult for many people to be unemotional about decisions involving money, many set up automated programs to help manage risk. The advantage is that the computer makes the trade using your predetermined price points, leaving your emotions out of the decision. The disadvantage is that at times, you may not get a competitive price. Let's take a brief look at the ways you can use automation to reduce risk.

Use Stop Losses

I believe in using stop loss orders (remember, this is an advance order that instructs the broker to enter an order to sell or buy when the price falls or rises to a designated level). Whether you're an investor or trader, they're an essential tool to help keep small losses from becoming big ones. Using stop losses is similar to performing a high-wire act with a safety net.

The stop loss is the net, and when used properly, it limits risk. Although stop losses are very helpful, the stop loss *market order* can cause occasional problems. In fact, when you set a stop loss market order, you are basically letting the market take control of your order. The advantage of any market order is that it will get filled quickly. On many occasions, however, you will receive a less competitive price.

Therefore, if you are going to use a stop loss, either use a mental stop loss (where you must enter the order manually), or use a stop loss *limit order* (you enter two prices: one setting a ceiling on the amount you'll pay for a stock, the other setting a floor at which you'll sell a stock). The traditional stop loss market order is not recommended because when prices are changing quickly, as in a fast market, you could get your order filled at a terrible price.

Nevertheless, you must find a system that works for you. If you are not able to monitor the market on a regular basis, the stop loss market order may work for you. Just realize that it is not perfect.

Use Stop Loss Alerts

An excellent way of monitoring positions is to set up alerts on your mobile device or computer. Nearly every brokerage firm allows this, or you can download stock-tracking apps (i.e., applications) for your mobile devices from the Internet. (A list of free stock trading apps appears in Chapter 14.)

There are a lot of advantages to using automated alerts for the various indexes. If the stock (or index) goes above or below a certain price level, you will be notified by text message or e-mail. Then you can choose to ignore the alert or to take action. This puts control back in your hands rather than depending on the computer.

It's simple to set up alerts. The hard part, as always, is having the discipline to act on them.

Protection Strategies

Another way to reduce risk is by protecting your portfolio. The following are a couple of strategies you can use if you want to protect the value of your stocks or index funds. These are for experienced investors or traders, but everyone should learn how to use them.

Buy Protective Puts

Buying put options makes sense if you are not certain that a bull market will continue. Owning puts will limit, but not eliminate, risk against large losses. Keep in mind that buying call or put options for protection is like buying expensive insurance. Most of the time the insurance expires and becomes worthless, but it does provide at least partial protection against something bad happening.

As we discussed previously, put options gain in value as stocks decline. For example, let's say you own the SPY ETF (a bullish position), which tracks the performance of the S&P 500 index. If you own a SPY put option and SPY falls, then the value of your option will rise (similar to buying an inverse ETF). The more SPY falls, the more valuable your put option becomes. Basically, your put is acting as insurance, limiting your losses.

Buying protective puts is primarily for people who fear a decline but still want to hold their bullish position. On the other hand, if your observation of market indicators suggests that a market decline is imminent, the easiest solution is to sell your shares and avoid unnecessary complications.

Although buying puts for protection is sometimes a good idea, it has some disadvantages. Remember that insurance is not free, and puts can be costly. If your shares move modestly higher and the entire sum spent on puts becomes worthless, you may be annoyed that you gave up all or most of your profits to buy those puts. Also, puts don't provide 100 percent protection against loss. Although they do limit risk, you may not be pleased with the size of the loss.

That is the choice you have to make: to buy put protection or sell some of your positions. In the event of a bear market or a crash, puts can be your friend.

Bottom Line

Put options tend to be expensive; for this reason a better strategy is to scale out of a portion of your holdings when the bull market is losing strength but is not yet bearish enough to sell everything. Ultimately it's your decision, but scaling out of a position is preferable to constantly buying put options. As you know, I discuss a variety of bullish and bearish options strategies in my book *Understanding Options* (McGraw-Hill, 2nd edition).

Diversify

Most investors are aware of the principle behind diversification, but few use it properly. Diversification is the mantra that financial experts chant, and it is designed to protect you from nasty downturns. The idea is to have a mix of stocks in various market sectors (e.g., transportation, health, technology) as well as in other asset classes (e.g., bonds, commodities, international stocks). Simply put, diversification means that you are betting on a number of potential outcomes. If one segment of the market crashes, since you are not putting all of your eggs in one basket, your risk is contained.

Theoretically, diversification works. Some sectors always perform better than others. Thus, holding stocks in different sectors acts as a hedge, and reduces losses when the market declines. One of the advantages of index ETFs and index funds is that they provide instant diversification.

Unfortunately, one of the mistakes some investors make is being overdiversified. Instead of keeping it simple with a handful of index ETFs or index funds, they may overdo it by owning too many stocks or mutual funds. Overdiversification may cancel any potential profits, and erode the ability of your investments to outperform the market. Hint: Focus on the quality of your investments rather than on the quantity.

Finally, while diversification is designed to reduce risk, it does not eliminate it completely. Often you do not know you are not diversified until after you have lost money, and by then it's too late. There is no standard diversification formula because it depends on how much risk you are comfortable with, your financial goals, and your time horizon. Nevertheless, if you stick with the indexes (and follow the strategies in this book), you should be properly diversified.

Advice to Novice Investors: Start Small

If you're a beginner, you must recognize that it's easy to lose money in the market. Therefore, when you're ready to place that first trade, start with fewer dollars—that is, start small. Obviously, "small" is a relative term that depends on the size of your account and net worth. Nevertheless, if you have never placed a trade, use no more than 3 to 5 percent of your account in one position.

Why so little? Your primary concern is to learn about the market and, most important, to minimize the chances of losing money. In other words, you want to survive (especially if you want to trade stocks). Bad habits are difficult to break; if a new trader thinks that "it's only a small amount of money so I'll take my chances," that attitude is likely to carry over when trading even larger positions. Entering small is all about risk management, and it's the best path for successful traders.

Your goal is to develop good habits right now. It is not the total dollars at risk that is important. The important part is the percentage of your holdings that are at risk. Certainly, losing $200 may not seem like a huge amount, but if your account is only $1,000, that represents 20 percent, which is a good-sized loss for any investor.

At first, become comfortable with entering buy and sell orders as well as learning about the tools discussed in this book. Although you may want to start with individual stocks, it's better to begin with an ETF such as SPY, which tracks the performance of 500 U.S. stocks. As you have already learned, only buy this investment if you believe the market is in a bullish environment.

As a beginner, you are going to make mistakes and lose money— virtually everyone does. By starting with a small dollar amount, you can build your confidence, study the market, and learn how to evaluate underlying conditions. As you gain experience, you can always increase the amount of your investments.

I want to applaud you for making it this far. I hope my book has been educational and entertaining. The next chapter has a little more advice for you.

CHAPTER 13

Sincere Advice

Here we'll tie everything together: the bull and bear investing philosophy outlined in this book. If you are new to the stock market, this chapter will be very educational. If you're an experienced investor, think of this as a review.

Sit Tight

As you know by now, making money in the stock market is deceptively easy during bull markets but a bit challenging in bear markets. At this point, you should feel more comfortable about managing positions in both environments.

If you choose to participate in the market, you'll learn that it has no intention of making your financial life easier. On the one hand, it seems quite simple because the market can only move up, down, or sideways. On the other hand, there's much more to successful investing than buy, hold, or sell.

When you're an investor, sometimes you just have to wait before your chosen strategy can be successful. As you know, it's the sitting and waiting that's difficult for most people. But the more you study the market, the more you realize that it really has a personality. If you can make the market your friend (even if the friendship is one-sided because it will never be loyal to you), investing becomes much easier. Follow along when it's in a good mood, and avoid it when it's angry. Obviously, it's a little more complicated than that, but not by much.

You can make money in the market by using simple strategies. They're understandable and easy to use, and they're just common sense. And now, I'd like to introduce the simple indexing strategy I use.

My Investing Strategy

Consider my indexing strategy as a starting point because your ultimate goal is to create your own strategy. You don't want to depend on anyone to tell you how to invest.

Market conditions change rapidly, so my strategy may also change in the future. In fact, every strategy can be tweaked and improved upon. With those caveats, here's my strategy, which reflects exactly what you've read so far:

In a bull market, I buy ETFs of the major market indexes such as SPY, IWM, QQQ, and DIA. In a bear market, I like to buy SH, RWM, and DOG. When the market is not moving very far in either direction (it's a sideways market), I increase my cash holdings.

Even during bull markets I keep some cash on the side. At times, I speculate with call and put options. During bull markets, I also use short-term trading tactics with a few individual stocks.

As you can see, I rarely buy individual stocks anymore, and I do not buy and hold indefinitely. I use the indicators and clues discussed in this book to monitor the overall market. If I can stay one step ahead of the market, I consider that a success.

In fact, being one step behind isn't so bad either. The point is not to fall too far behind. I often sell too soon when I detect a dangerous market, but I will sit and wait until the danger has passed. I never pick tops or bottoms, because trying to do so is a money-losing strategy, in my opinion.

In front of my computer I have small, color-coded index cards with "bull" (green), "bear" (red), or "sideways" (yellow) written on them. I look at them at least once every day. This helps me to stick to my market index strategies, and not get scared out of a position simply because the market had a one- or two-day reversal.

In addition, I follow a handful of indicators such as the AAII and Investor's Intelligence sentiment surveys, put/call ratio, VIX, the moving averages (50-day, 100-day, and 200-day), MACD, RSI, and the 10-year Treasury yield.

By monitoring the market with these tools, I get a good idea of which direction the financial winds are blowing. There are hundreds of different indicators, so you have to find the ones that produce winning results for you. These are the ones I like, however, and I'm sure I'll add to and subtract from this list in the future.

Market Mastery

Another strategy that I use is to have a core position in the index funds and then use a small portion of my portfolio to speculate with certain individual stocks or options. That takes a little more work. Although you can buy and hold the indexes without worrying too much about the day-to-day fluctuations, with many individual stocks and options you have to monitor the position closely.

How Investors Come Up Short

When it comes to the stock market, we are our own worst enemy. Investors get too emotional about the market, buy stocks on margin at all-time highs, and dump everything near market lows in a selling panic. As long as there is a stock market, investors and traders will do what feels right at the moment but is wrong in retrospect. Many of the biggest mistakes occur with individual stocks, which is why buying indexes is less risky.

If you follow the advice in this book and stick with trading the indexes, you can do very well in the market (although there are no guarantees).

Your goal, as you know by now, is to match the indexes during bull markets and avoid being invested during bear markets. If you follow this strategy and are patient and consistent, you will build wealth over time.

Unfortunately, what no one can teach you is discipline—you have to learn it for yourself. It is the lack of discipline that results in losses and portfolio destruction. In the heat of battle, as the market is either exploding higher or crashing, many people throw away their strategies, plans, and trading rules and follow their instincts. That is almost always the wrong move.

Avoid following your instincts (unless you are a professional investor), and learn a strategy well. When you are confident that you understand how it works and what to do during all market situations, follow that strategy and your trade plan. Use the guidelines included in this book, and create your own rules (and write them down).

The Rules

When you have a detailed plan that is written in advance, you don't have to worry that fear or greed will interfere with your trades. If you are trading indexes, most of the essential rules are included in this book. If you decide to trade individual stocks, however, take the time to review the following rules. (You may also learn a few things from them if you trade indexes.) Nevertheless, eventually you want to create your own set of rules. My role here is to get you started on the right path.

Rule #1: Create Three Prices before Placing a Trade— Enter, Exit, and Escape

If you are going to trade, it's essential that you use the three E's—that is, decide on three prices in advance: an entry price, an exit price, and an escape price. Before placing your order, it's important to think of these three prices.

- **Entry Price:** This is your preferred buy price. You may not get it, but it is your goal. If the current price is too high and you don't want to pay this price, then enter a good-'til-canceled order to purchase at your desired price. Before you enter the information, be certain that you still want to buy those shares at that price.
- **Exit Price:** This is your ideal selling price. Before buying a stock, know why you are buying it. That means that you should have one of two plans in mind:

  1. Plan A: This is a long-term investment. You will re-evaluate the worthiness of this investment at least once per month. Under this plan, you do not have a specific sale price.
  2. Plan B: You bought this stock to earn a short-term profit. If you do not have a specific profit goal in mind, then ask yourself why you are buying the stock. Choose an exit price based on profit or on technical levels such as moving averages. If you choose a percentage gain, make sure it is realistic.

Too many people are eager to buy but never give any thought to the sale price. Writing down a desired exit price helps you lock in gains. It also helps prevent a winning stock from turning into a loser. Although you want to let your winners run, there is nothing wrong with taking some money off the table. By establishing an exit price, you will do just that.

- **Escape Price:** This is an emergency sell price, what traders call a stop loss price. Even when you trade indexes, it's a good idea to establish a written price where you will decide whether to hold or exit.

    For example, if the market suddenly sells off, and your stock is down by more than 5 percent, this is a warning sign. If this happens during a bull market, then the time may be right to sell this underperforming stock and replace it with a better performing stock. After all, you do not want to hold laggards when the market is rising.

There should also be a specific price level when you sell and don't look back. (I call it the "5 percent rule," but I may not sell until the loss reaches 7 or 8 percent.)

The reasons for creating entry, exit, and escape prices are to minimize losses, lock in profits, and, most of all, avoid making impulsive decisions during the trading day. The biggest danger to your trading account is ignoring a small loss that then grows into an unacceptably larger loss. That is why it's essential that you know the price level, or the dollar loss, at which you will take action. That becomes your trading plan. By writing down these prices in advance, it will be much easier for you to follow the plan rather than your emotions.

Rule #2: Avoid Trading During the First Fifteen Minutes of the Trading Day

If you are a beginner, you may want to avoid the first fifteen minutes after the market opens. Occasionally there's a lot of action at that time because panicked buyers and sellers are placing their orders. Also, orders from the night before are being processed.

During these extreme conditions, the market can move in one direction and then reverse direction shortly after the opening. It's easy for a novice investor to get caught up in the emotional opening and lose money when the market changes direction. If you are eager to trade in those first fifteen minutes, you have to ask yourself why. Why is it so important to place the trade as soon as the market opens? In fact, making those impulsive trades first thing in the morning often results in losses.

If you're going to place a trade, do it when you are unemotional. At the market open after the bell rings, enthusiasm is often high. Once the market calms down after fifteen or twenty minutes, then you can look for something to buy or sell.

On the other hand, if you're an experienced short-term trader, the market open can provide profitable trading opportunities. For example, gap openings (when the market moves violently in either direction) may occur during the first fifteen minutes.

Rule #3: Use Limit Orders, Not Market Orders

This is one of those rules many people learn the hard way. When you place a market order, you are telling your broker to buy or sell at the "best available price." Unfortunately, that doesn't mean the most competitive price. When you place a market order, you are telling the brokerage computer to make the trade immediately, regardless of the price.

The main advantage of using a market order is speed. The order is filled immediately. But ask yourself how quickly you need that order filled. Limit orders make a lot more sense, and will probably save money.

With the limit order, you specify the price at which you are willing to buy or sell. Your order is filled when the stock reaches the price you specify. Because you set the parameters, you always get that price, or better. For example, if you enter a limit price to sell

XYZ at $20 per share, then XYZ will not be sold unless your price is at least $20.00.

On the other hand, if you used a market order, it's possible that your order will be filled at a very poor price. Here's a worst-case example: Let's say that you entered a market order to sell XYZ at $20 per share. If there were a flash crash (which is rare), or even a volatile market, instead of getting your order filled at $20, it could be filled at a price much less than $20 per share, depending on market conditions. When you use a market order, you have given the market full control of your order. Most of the time, it's not a problem, but during unusual market conditions, market orders can cost you money.

Bottom Line

Get in the habit of using limit orders.

Rule #4: Don't Go on Margin

Margin allows traders to borrow money from their brokers. Most brokerages have a 2:1 margin rate, which means that if you have $5,000 in stocks or cash, you are allowed to borrow an additional $5,000 to purchase more stock. Margin offers extra buying power.

Margin works great when stocks are going up and you are making a profit. The problem with using it is that if your stocks go down, losses accelerate. Leverage is a two-way street, and when the market is going the wrong way, it's painful.

A "margin call" occurs when the brokerage notifies you that you no longer have sufficient assets in your account. Remember that when using margin, you are borrowing money from your broker, and the margin call alerts you to the fact that the broker requires more cash. Failure to deposit that cash in a timely manner will result in the broker selling some of your holdings to generate the needed cash. (Margin rules are set by the Securities and Exchange

Commission; each individual broker is allowed to require more cash than the SEC requires, but never less.)

If you are going to trade stocks, you must be realistic. Don't put yourself in a position where you could lose more money than you have in your account. In the case of a market correction, or even a bad earnings report, the use of margin can wipe out your account. Overall, as a new investor you are better off not using margin, though professional traders do use it to increase buying power.

Rule #5: Create Time Targets

Many beginners spend their time thinking of the stocks they want to buy (and worse, what they're going to do with the profits) but never consider when to sell. In addition to setting price targets, think about time targets. A time target means reviewing your purchase after a certain amount of time. If the stock is not performing, you must have a good reason for not selling.

Most people have limited capital to use for investments. If money is tied up with a dud stock, it is earning nothing; at some point, you will need to think of finding a replacement. The main point is that you want a selling plan that includes both price and time targets, and they should be written down.

Before you buy a stock, be certain to create a trading plan. In your plan, you will have realistic price targets (a 100 percent gain is not realistic), as well as reasonable time targets (holding forever is not a selling strategy, nor is playing it by ear).

Rule #6: Keep a Trade Journal

Most successful traders keep detailed records of their winning and losing trades. Writing down what you did, both right and wrong, helps teach you to be a better trader. In particular, by listing and analyzing your mistakes, you will improve as a trader.

With a journal, you will discover which trades cause you the most trouble. When you recognize that, it is easy to avoid making similar trades in the future (as well as steering clear of mistakes). For example, perhaps you constantly sell your winners too early. Or perhaps you make impulsive trades, forget to use a stop loss, and then lose money. By writing the details in the journal, you will be less likely to repeat the same mistakes, or bad trades, that you made in the past.

Rule #7: Practice in a Paper Trading Account

Before entering the market for the first time, it's a good idea to create a practice trading account. Of course, some will argue that the only way to experience the true pain of losing money and the stress of decision-making is by investing real money. On the other hand, practice trading allows you to learn to make decisions, keep records, enter orders, and make a trade plan. It gives you an opportunity to make trade decisions and try different strategies without fear of losing real money. For those who take it seriously, paper trading can be a helpful tool. Most brokers allow paper trading. If yours does not, many other Internet sites do.

Rule #8: Trust Your Own Judgment

One of the greatest lessons you will learn when managing your own account is that you have no one to blame when you make a mistake. At first it can be a little intimidating to rely on your own judgment. However, doing so is one of the greatest gifts you can give to yourself. It means that you no longer have to listen to bad advice or let other people make mistakes (or succeed) on your behalf. Instead, you must do your own research—though admittedly this takes more work. The best part: When trusting your own judgment, instead of trading for a day you can trade for a lifetime.

Rule #9: Cut Your Losses

To survive as a trader, you must know how to sell a losing stock. Don't make excuses, don't hope the stock will recover, and don't blame the market. If the stock is not performing as expected, you must cut it out of your portfolio and never look back. Once a stock hits your escape price or no longer performs as expected, sell it.

Rule #10: Learn How to Lose

If you're new to the stock market, this is a difficult rule to follow. After all, most of us grow up thinking we must always win. But when it comes to the stock market, it's okay to have losses, as long as you keep those losses small (which is why you cut your losing stocks at 7 or 8 percent, if not sooner).

When the market goes in the wrong direction, many novice traders make panic trades. Do not panic if you have losses. If you trade stocks, you must be willing to accept some losing trades, along with the gains.

If you do lose money, try not to get trapped into the "woulda, coulda, shoulda" syndrome. Even worse, many people constantly complain that "if only" they had bought Google (or Boeing or Wal-mart) when it was first listed for trading, they could have made a fortune.

Rather than complaining about the mistakes you made in the past, work on being a better trader in the future. Everyone has a "woulda, coulda, shoulda" story, and there's nothing we can do about it anymore. What we *can* do is make sure that the next trade will be a smart one with a good chance to earn a profit.

Rule #11: Find Out for Yourself What Works

When investing in the market, it's difficult to know which stocks to sell and which stocks to hold. It's easy to go back and be a Monday morning quarterback. With hindsight it's easy to say which stocks you should have bought or sold.

Therefore, you need to go out on your own and find out what works for you. Not for me, or anyone else, but for you. The only way you can do that is by actually trading. As long as you start small (with a small percentage of your trading account), you can test different strategies, accept losses, and find out which of the ideas in this book actually work. Just remember that the main idea is to be invested during bull markets and on the sidelines during bear markets.

In the future, the stock market will undergo changes. There will be new technologies and more efficient ways to trade. As you go forward from here, take the time to learn as much as you can about the stock market.

As I've suggested, you may avoid trading stocks and stick to trading indexes. Others who read this book may find that indexes are too boring and will try more speculative strategies. There is no right answer. The objective is to find out how to achieve your financial goals with the least amount of risk. In fact, you might discover that you don't want to be in the stock market at all. But the only way you can find out what works for you is by studying, testing, and trying out new things.

Finally, although it's not included as a rule, one of the most important characteristics for successful trading is being disciplined. It's one of those things that either you have or you have to work hard to develop. Discipline, along with flexibility, is essential if you are going to be a successful trader.

Anticipate Probabilities

Before the end of this chapter, let's look at one more Livermore story. He had bought and sold stocks his whole life, and amassed a multimillion-dollar fortune (three times). After trying every possible strategy, Livermore made another important discovery:

"Obviously, the thing to do was to be bullish in a bull market and bearish in a bear market. Sounds silly, doesn't it? But I had to grasp that general principle firmly before I saw that to put it into practice really meant to anticipate probabilities. It took me a long time to learn to trade on those lines."

This entire book is based on what Livermore said in this paragraph. In other words, evaluate underlying market conditions, follow the market trend, and anticipate the market's next move as well as the probability of that move.

CHAPTER 14

Where to Get Help

There aren't a lot of books about learning how to assess underlying market conditions. Nevertheless, the following books should be helpful if you want to expand on your knowledge about the stock market. I will add to this list in future editions.

Books

How to Make Money in Stocks (McGraw-Hill, 2009) by William J. O'Neil.
This ground-breaking book shows you how to profit in the market with a rule-based, systematic approach.

One Up on Wall Street (Simon & Schuster, 2000) by Peter Lynch and John Rothchild.
How to profit in the market using a long-term investment approach, which includes observing what people are buying at the mall or other stores, and knowing the companies before you buy their stock.

The Little Book of Common Sense Investing (Wiley, 2007) by John Bogle.
This is an excellent book written by the creator of the first index fund. Bogle makes a strong case for why you should buy and hold

index funds. If you like indexing, you can thank John Bogle for being far ahead of his time.

Reminiscences of a Stock Operator (Wiley Investment Classics, 2006) by Edwin Lefevre.

A must-read classic about the trading experiences of Jesse Livermore, a legendary trader from the early twentieth century.

Market Wizards, 2nd edition (Wiley, 2012) and *The New Market Wizards* (Harper Business, 1994) by Jack Schwager.

The author delves into the minds of profitable traders in these two classic books.

Useful Websites for Investors and Traders

*paid subscription required
www.aaii.com (AAII) *
www.barrons.com (Barrons) *
www.bigcharts.com (Big Charts)
www.bloomberg.com (Bloomberg)
www.briefing.com (Briefing)
www.cnbc.com (CNBC)
Finance.yahoo.com (Yahoo! Finance)
www.fool.com (Motley Fool) *
www.foxbusiness.com (Fox Business News)
www.forbes.com (*Forbes Magazine*)
www.ft.com (*Financial Times*) *
www.google.com/finance (Google Finance)
www.investopedia.com (Investopedia)
www.investors.com (*Investor's Business Daily*) *
www.kiplinger.com (*Kiplinger's*)
www.marketwatch.com (MarketWatch)

Money.cnn.com (Money)
www.money.msn.com (MSN Money)
www.moneyshow.com (The Money Show)
www.morningstar.com (Morningstar)
www.nasdaq.com (Nasdaq)
www.nyse.com (New York Stock Exchange)
www.quote.com (Quote.com)
www.sec.gov (SEC)
www.seekingalpha.com (Seeking Alpha)
www.stockcharts.com (StockCharts)
www.thestreet.com (The Street) *
www.valueline.com (Value Line) *
www.wsj.com (*Wall Street Journal*) *

Useful Apps

Note: Most of the previous websites listed have apps, although not all are free. All of the following apps listed below can be downloaded for free.

Associated Press
Bloomberg
MarketWatch
Real-Time Stocks
Reuters
Stock Tracker
Y! Finance

Now that you know where to get help, I have some closing remarks, as well as information on how to contact me.

What You Should Do Now

Congratulations! You finished the book. With the information it provided, I hope you will profit from bull markets, be protected from bear markets, and be prepared for every market. Most important, you have learned how to study the overall market and underlying conditions. In the future, wait for favorable conditions before making a trade.

I also hope that you see the market differently from before. Although it's a fascinating place, the market can be like a matrix at times. Like *The Matrix*, it's difficult to know what is real and what is an illusion. This book has helped you to see the difference.

Before you go, here are some final comments.

Never Stop Learning

The biggest mistake I made as a beginning trader was not buying an index ETF or index mutual fund. That would have saved me a lot of aggravation, not to mention money.

If you're a beginner, start with the indexes. When you gain more experience, you can use more strategies if you desire. But at the very least, have one broad-based market index in your portfolio.

If you're a college student, you're fortunate because you can start buying index funds early. You'll be amazed at how the magic of compounding interest can help you to build wealth over time.

If you're a parent, teach your children about the stock market. Help them start an investment account. Some schools have programs for middle school and high school students, but much more needs to be done. Children love the idea that instead of working for their money, their money is working for them. Learning the basics of the stock market and how to manage money are essential skills (and very important as they get older).

Invest in Yourself

Now that you are aware of the risks as well as the rewards of investing in the stock market, you have a choice. If you are willing to take the time to learn what works for you and your financial goals, you can survive and prosper as a twenty-first-century investor.

Fortunately, you have more tools and information than any investor had in the past. As soon as you put down this book, begin thinking and planning. Don't stop until you have created a successful trading plan, strategy, and investment portfolio. My advice is to keep it simple and to start small. Always be on the lookout for profitable moneymaking opportunities while remaining cautious. Rather than attempting to beat Mr. Market, one of your goals is to join him in the Winner's Circle.

Another goal is to build up enough confidence so that you can invest or trade independently. If you have the confidence to manage your own account, you will be able to invest for a lifetime and not depend on others for advice. You can listen to others, but you must think for yourself.

Finally, the best investment you can make is in people. You can't go wrong spending money on an education, a home, a new business, your children, or those who desperately need your help. After all, why make money if you don't use it to improve your life or the lives of others?

It's been a pleasure sharing my knowledge and experiences with you, and I wish that all your financial dreams come true. Before I go, I'd like to share with you a letter written by my grandfather, Charles Sincere (a *Wall Street Journal* article with similar advice was attached to the letter).

The letter contained the following financial advice to his son (my father):

1. "Begin by paying off all your debts.
2. "After being debt-free, you must not be tempted to blow your money on risky financial ventures.
3. "It is hard enough for most people to earn a bare living, including 95 percent who are unable to keep and acquire a fortune. This is not to discourage you but to warn you and give you courage to fight harder to be one of the 5 percent.
4. "Always be prepared for the possibility that you may have to support your parents. In addition, you owe it to your wife and family to buy life insurance.
5. "You want the privilege of helping those who are afflicted and impoverished.
6. "The most important measure of success is integrity, hard work, and being right more than 55 percent of the time. This also means diversifying risks so that when you are wrong it won't break or crimp you.
7. "Never cosign promissory notes to help others.
8. "Never buy stocks in small corporations to please friends— easy to buy, hard to sell.
9. "Don't be easy in loaning money except in extreme cases (i.e., don't let a worthy friend down).
10. "Only hard experience, proven by facts, should impress you and cause you to follow the rules just outlined."

Good luck!

Glossary

10-year Treasury (Symbol: ^TNX):
The Chicago Board Options Exchange (CBOE) Interest Rate
10-year Treasury Note is a bond issued by the U.S. government at a
fixed rate that pays interest once every six months. The yield on the
10-year Treasury moves in the opposite direction of bond prices.

American Association of Individual Investors (AAII):
A nonprofit educational organization that polls its members
each week for their view of the market bullish, bearish, or neutral.

Ask price (or offer):
The current lowest price that a seller is willing to accept for an
individual security.

Bear market:
A stock market environment in which investors are gloomy,
the prices of stocks and other securities are falling, and the broad
market indexes have fallen by 20 percent or more off its recent high.

Bid price:
The highest price a buyer is willing to pay for an individual
security. Also, the price that a seller will receive when selling "at the
market."

Black swan:
An unexpected and extreme event that can cause a violent downward market move.

Bond:
A type of loan issued by a government, local municipality, or company in order to raise capital.

Bubble:
An economic condition in which an asset (stock market, commodity, etc.) climbs well above its true value so that it is no longer based on fundamental conditions. Instead, investor exuberance leads to ever-increasing prices. Every bubble eventually pops when reality penetrates investors' minds.

Bull market:
A stock market environment in which investors are optimistic and the prices of stocks, indexes, and other assets are rising.

Buy-and-hold:
An investment strategy in which an investor buys stocks and holds them indefinitely, regardless of short-term fluctuations in the market.

Call option:
A financial contract that gives buyers the right, but not the obligation, to buy an asset by a certain date at a certain price.

Capitulation:
A situation when a huge number of investors suddenly give up any hope that the stock market will stop falling. They sell their stocks or other assets in a panic. The ensuing large volume drives prices to fall even more quickly, eventually forming a bottom.

Chart pattern:

A repeating and recognizable pattern that occurs in market charts when plots of financial data are created. Chart patterns may help predict future price movements. The double bottom, double top, or head and shoulders are examples of stock chart patterns.

Chicago Board Options Exchange Market Volatility Index (VIX):

A market indicator that measures the implied volatility of specific options on SPX, the S&P 500 Index. It is considered to be a measure of fear and complacency among market participants.

Consumer Price Index (CPI):

An economic indicator, published monthly by the U.S. Bureau of Labor Statistics, that is used to identify deflationary or inflationary trends.

Correction:

A temporary decline in the broad-based market indexes.

Crash:

A large and often rapid decline in stock prices brought on when many investors simultaneously enter orders to sell their holdings. As a result, buyers are overwhelmed, or disappear altogether. The selling panic results in a further plunge in the prices of the major market indexes, usually by at least a double-digit percentage.

Diversification:

A strategy where an investor owns a variety of assets to reduce risk. In theory, if one asset goes down, another in the portfolio will move higher.

Dollar cost averaging:
An investment strategy involving the purchase of a fixed dollar amount of a stock or other security on a regular, recurring basis. For example, buy $100 of XYZ stock every two weeks.

Dow Jones Industrial Average (DJIA):
A price-weighted average of thirty blue-chip stocks that trade on the New York and Nasdaq stock exchanges.

Downtrend:
A period when the overall direction or movement of a security's price is lower.

Exchange-traded fund (ETF):
A basket of assets (for example, stocks) that trades on a stock exchange and tracks an index, commodity, or currency.

Federal Reserve (the Fed):
The central banking system of the United States, created in 1913, and responsible for overseeing money supply, interest rates, and credit.

Flash crash:
A very rapid, very short-lived, and large market decline. One occurred on May 6, 2010, when the Dow plunged by more than 1,000 points within minutes, only to recover the losses that same day. Blame was placed on an errant E-mini option futures trader whose keyboard error resulted in placing an order that was far larger than intended.

Fundamental analysis:
A method of evaluating a stock or other security by examining the underlying business such as data in the financial statements, competitors, and management.

Good-'Til-Canceled (GTC):
An instruction to a broker to keep a buy or sell order active until it has been filled, even if it takes weeks or years. Some brokers automatically cancel such orders after ninety days.

High-frequency trading (HFT):
A trading method where computers generate a huge number of buy and sell orders. The trading strategy uses complex algorithms to find trades with very short (microseconds-long) holding periods, and with profits as low as a fraction of one penny.

Index ETFs:
A basket of stocks designed to track the performance of a specific market index. Rather than buy every stock in an index, investors buy ETFs such as SPY (tracks S&P 500), DIA (tracks Dow Jones Industrial Average), QQQ (tracks Nasdaq-100), and IWM (tracks Russell 2000) instead.

Index mutual fund:
A basket of stocks designed to track the performance of a specific index such as the S&P 500. Such funds have very low management fees. The Vanguard 500 Index Fund is one example.

Inverse ETFs:
A basket of stocks that tracks the performance of the inverse of a specific index or underlying benchmark. For example, when the underlying index goes down, the inverse ETF goes up. This is equivalent to owning a basket in which every stock in the index

is sold short. Examples of inverse ETFs include DOG (inverse of Dow Jones Industrial Average), SH (inverse of S&P 500), RWM (inverse of Russell 2000), and PSQ (inverse of Nasdaq-100).

Investors Intelligence:
A sentiment survey, published by Chartcraft, that polls over 100 independent financial newsletter writers for their view of the market.

Lagging indicator:
A technical indicator that follows, or lags, the price of an underlying security.

Leverage:
A technique whereby borrowed capital is used to multiply gains or losses, thereby increasing (or decreasing) the investment return.

Leveraged ETF:
An investment basket that magnifies (by two or three times) the daily performance of an underlying index by using financial derivatives and other products. Primarily designed for short-term traders, leveraged ETFs should not be held more than a day or two.

Limit order:
An order to buy or sell an asset at a specific price or better.

Liquidity:
A measure of how quickly a trader can get into (buy) or out of (sell) a security at the same price level.

Long position:
A position held by an investor hoping to profit when the price goes up.

Margin account:

A type of brokerage account where a customer can borrow cash (to gain leverage) from the brokerage to buy securities.

Margin call:

A message from a brokerage firm to a customer, demanding the immediate deposit of enough cash to satisfy maintenance requirements (and the Federal Reserve Board rule, Regulation T), for owning an investment. The idea is to protect the broker against losses resulting from an unfavorable price movement.

Market indicator:

Statistical data (technical, fundamental, sentiment, or economic) that may provide clues and insights into future market direction.

Market order:

An order to buy or sell a stock at the best available price.

Mental stop:

A stop loss order that is not actually entered by a trader until the stop price is reached; at that point the order is entered.

Moving Average Convergence/Divergence (MACD):

A trend-following market indicator that helps determine when a trend has ended or begun, or may be reversing direction.

Moving averages:

The average of a number of data points (e.g., closing stock prices) derived as follows: Each day the oldest point is removed, replaced by the most recent, and a new average is calculated and plotted on a chart. Typically 50-, 100-, or 200-day moving averages are used for stocks. Commonly used to smooth out short-term fluctuations and highlight longer-term trends.

Mutual fund:
A basket of stocks managed by professional fund managers using pooled money from many investors to buy the assets being managed.

Nasdaq-100:
An index of 100 of the largest nonfinancial companies listed on the Nasdaq-100 stock market exchange.

Nasdaq Composite:
An index containing more than 3,000 stocks traded on the Nasdaq stock exchange. These stocks include technology corporations such as Google, Facebook, and Apple.

Nasdaq Stock Exchange:
The first electronic stock exchange, National Association of Securities Dealers Automated Quotations.

Net asset value (NAV):
The value of one share of a mutual fund, based on its assets less its liabilities. It is calculated at the close of business each day.

New York Stock Exchange (NYSE):
One of the largest stock exchanges in the world, the NYSE is located at 11 Wall Street in New York.

No-load:
A mutual fund that has no sales charge (i.e., front-end load). For most investors, no-load mutual funds are preferable because they are less expensive.

Option:

A contract that gives its owner the right, but not the obligation, to buy or sell an underlying security at a specific price for a specific time period.

Overbought:

A condition when demand for a security is so high that it is not supported by fundamental data.

Oversold:

A condition when demand for a security is so low that it is not supported by fundamental data.

Parabolic:

A chart pattern that shows an asset's price moving up so fast and high that it appears to be going straight up. Inevitably, a parabolic stock or index reaches a climax, and then collapses.

Price to Earnings ratio (P/E ratio, or P/E):

A popular fundamental indicator, it is the stock price divided by its earnings per share. It can be used to compare whether a particular stock or index is a good value.

Pullback:

The downward reversal (often temporary) of a prolonged upward price trend.

Put option:

A financial contract that gives the buyer the right, but not the obligation, to sell an asset at a certain price by a certain date.

Pyramiding:
An investment strategy created by Jesse Livermore that involves making a number of purchases at key entry points as a stock continues to rise. Investors increase position size by using unrealized profits from successful trades to boost margin.

Relative Strength Indicator (RSI):
This helps to determine when the market or an individual security is overbought or oversold.

Resistance:
A price level where sellers previously prevented a stock from rising higher.

Reversal:
A change in the direction of a price trend.

Russell 2000:
An index of 2,000 small-cap stocks consisting of the smallest 2,000 stocks in the Russell 3000 index.

Scaling:
Buying or selling in increments as the price rises or falls.

Securities and Exchange Commission (SEC):
A government commission established by Congress and with members appointed by the U.S. president to regulate the securities markets and protect investors from fraud and manipulation.

Security:
A tradable investment instrument, such as a stock, bond, or option.

Share:
A unit of ownership issued to shareholders by a corporation.

Shorting (sell short):
The strategy of borrowing and selling shares of stock from a brokerage firm with the intention of buying them back later at a lower price.

Short position:
A position in which a stock was sold first with the anticipation of repurchasing later at a lower price. (See Shorting.)

Sideways market:
A range-bound market, which can be volatile or flat, where the broad-based indexes do not break through support or resistance, and no new multi-month highs or lows are made.

Small-cap stock:
Corporations with a small market capitalization worth between $300 million and $2 billion.

Standard & Poor's 500 Index (S&P 500):
A theoretical basket of stocks consisting of the 500 highest capitalized stocks that trade in the United States.

Stock market:
A place where investors' representatives (brokers) meet to buy and sell shares of stock. Today, the meeting (i.e., transaction) is arranged via computer, and seldom done face-to-face.

Stop loss limit order:
An order that is both a stop order and a limit order. The order is entered at a specified price (or better), but only after the stop is

triggered (i.e., the stock trades at, or through, the stop price). Once the stop is triggered, this order becomes a limit order to buy (or sell) at the limit price or better.

Stop loss market order:

An order that instructs a broker to buy or sell a stock "at the market" when it reaches the stop price. Designed to limit losses, the order is not ideal in a fast-moving market.

Support:

The price level where buyers previously prevented a stock from falling further.

Technical analysis:

A method of evaluating securities and attempting to anticipate future stock prices based on studying market data, including price and volume.

Uptrend:

A period when the overall direction or movement of a security is up.

Volatility:

The rate at which a security moves up or down over a period of time.

Volume:

The number of shares of a security traded during a certain period, usually one day.

Online and Discount Brokers

If you are a novice investor, you might wonder how to get started investing in the stock market. You start by choosing a brokerage firm. To help get started, I compiled a list of a few of the most popular online discount brokerage firms. These brokerage firms are primarily for self-directed traders since they offer little or no investment advice but do have excellent customer support desks. In addition, these firms offer fast execution of orders, sophisticated charting capabilities, and independent research.

Because brokerage firms occasionally merge or change names, to find an updated list of reputable brokerage firms, go on the Internet and do a search (suggested search words: "rank online brokerage firms," followed by the current year). A list of articles will appear from independent sources such as *Smart Money*, *Barron's*, and other periodicals that rank brokerage firms.

Here is a list of online brokerage firms:

E*Trade
www.etrade.com
E*Trade has excellent customer service, powerful trading tools, excellent research, a low minimum amount to open an account, free streaming quotes, and a large variety of investment products including mutual funds.

Fidelity Investments

www.fidelity.com

Fidelity has excellent customer service, a huge selection of investment products including mutual funds and ETFs, sophisticated trading and investment screens including streaming quotes, extensive research capabilities, and the ability to trade stocks from other countries. They are geared to active traders as well as investors. They have many local branch offices.

Charles Schwab & Co. (and OptionsXpress)

www.schwab.com

Schwab has many investment products including mutual funds with a low minimum investment. Customer service is excellent as is their research department. They are geared toward investors rather than traders. They have many local branch offices.

Scottrade

www.scottrade.com

Scottrade has excellent customer service, sophisticated trading tools, low fees, free streaming quotes for traders, a large variety of mutual funds, and a low minimum amount to open an account. They have many local branch offices.

TDAmeritrade (and ThinkOrSwim for active traders)

www.tdameritrade.com

TDAmeritrade has excellent customer service, low fees, a variety of investment products including mutual funds, independent research, and a powerful trading platform. They are geared for investors and traders, and has many local branch offices. Active traders can use the ThinkOrSwim platform.

TradeKing (and Zecco)
www.tradeking.com

Trade King has top-notch customer service, low fees and commissions, great mobile trading applications, real-time quotes, and a platform that is geared for both investors and traders.

Investment Publications

Before investing in the market I suggest that you do your homework, that is, read financial books and periodicals. Reading books and periodicals is a good place to learn more about the stock market.

The following are a few of the most popular resources, but there are many more (look in Chapter 14 for additional resources).

Barron's
www.barrons.com
This weekly financial newspaper, published by Dow Jones & Company, was founded in 1921. It focuses on stock market statistics and market activity, news reports, and business news. A popular feature is the annual *Barron's* Roundtable, where market experts make predictions about the stock market. Each year, *Barron's* also ranks the top online brokerage firms.

Financial Times
www.financialtimes.com
This paper, founded in 1888, is a British language newspaper that focuses on business and economic news. It is especially useful for checking world news and events.

Investor's Business Daily

www.investors.com

Founded in 1984 by William J. O'Neil, *Investor's Business Daily* provides detailed information and statistics about stocks, mutual funds, and commodities. Much of the stock charts and information reflects the investment philosophy of O'Neil, CAN SLIM.

Kiplinger's Personal Finance

www.kiplinger.com

Kiplinger's Personal Finance magazine contains personal finance articles that focus on making and saving money and building wealth by investing for the long term.

Money (CNN Money)

www.money.com

Owned by Time Warner, Inc., *Money* is an online magazine that includes personal finance articles that range from investing to saving for retirement.

Smart Money

www.smartmoney.com

Smart Money is a monthly personal finance magazine geared to investors, savers, and spenders.

ValueLine Investment Survey

www.valueline.com

Value Line is an investment research firm geared to investors who want detailed fundamental data about individual stocks and mutual funds.

Wall Street Journal

www.wallstreetjournal.com

Published by Dow Jones and Company, the *Wall Street Journal* is a leading international newspaper with a focus on economics, investment, and business topics. Founded in 1889, the *Wall Street Journal* has the largest circulation of any newspaper in the United States.

Online Investment Websites

One of the most efficient and easiest places to research stocks is the Internet. All of the brokerage firms have their own websites devoted to investing and trading. At a minimum, brokerage websites contain stock, option, and ETF quotes, charts, research, articles, and investment advice. A list of mutual funds and their current NAV will be displayed as well as fees and commissions. Once you sign up with a brokerage, you will be able to assess account information and be able to make trades online.

In addition to the brokerage websites, the following is a list of a few of the investment-related websites available to investors and traders.

Bloomberg News
www.bloomberg.com
On Bloomberg you can read breaking financial news, check quotes, read articles and opinion on stocks, mutual funds, ETFs, and currencies. It is an excellent resource for checking stock futures or overseas news and quotes. Bloomberg also has an informative financial television program, Bloomberg TV as well as a mobile app.

Briefing.com

www.briefing.com

Since 1993, Briefing.com has provided in-depth analysis and commentary of the U.S. and international markets. Their site is loaded with useful information such as stocks that are on the move, breaking news, an economic calendar, and informational articles. Most of the site is free but they also offer premium analysis for a monthly fee. Briefing.com is useful to both traders and investors.

CNBC

www.cnbc.com

Most people are familiar with the entertaining financial television program, CNBC TV, where guests discuss both sides of the market all day. They also have special features and market analysis from a variety of different sources. You can also watch the show on the Internet.

Fox Business

www.foxbusiness.com

Fox Business is on cable (and the Internet) and has a number of interesting guests who discuss the market and other financial news all day.

Google Finance

www.google.com/finance

Google Finance is a useful site that contains breaking news, stock screeners, simulated portfolios, charts, technical and fundamental indicators, and detailed quotes. It is easy to use and loaded with important information.

Investopedia

www.investopedia.com

Investopedia is an Internet site that started as a financial dictionary for investors and traders but has expanded to include tutorials, educational articles, videos, a popular mobile app, and a free stock market simulator using play money. The site contains information on stocks, options, and currencies.

MarketWatch

www.marketwatch.com

MarketWatch is a financial news website that provides market news, analysis, financial advice columns, and stock market data. You can use it to check breaking news in the U.S. or overseas. I write a monthly column for MarketWatch, "Michael Sincere's Long-Term Trader."

Morningstar

www.morningstar.com

Morningstar, an investment research firm, provides data for investors who need more information about mutual funds, ETFs, and stocks. They also have articles and news on their website and offer free as well as subscription-based products.

MSN Money

money.msn.com

MSN Money is a website that contains business news, quotes, and articles on stocks and personal finance.

Nasdaq

www.nasdaq.com

This is the website of the Nasdaq Stock Exchange, the first electronic exchange. They have real-time quotes, headline news, quotes, and research such as SEC filings and stock reports.

NYSE Euronext

www.nyse.nyx.com

This is the website of NYSE Euronext, which operates four stock and option exchanges across the U.S. and Europe. The most well known trading exchange is the New York Stock Exchange, which is located at 11 Wall Street.

Options Industry Council (OIC)

www.optionseducation.org

The OIC is the place to go if you need to learn more about options. They have tools, option trading simulators, webinars, podcasts, online and live seminars, articles, and a help line to answer option questions.

Quote.com

www.quote.com

Quote.com has detailed stock quotes, charts, financial news, and commentary.

StockCharts.com

www.stockcharts.com

StockCharts not only has detailed stock quotes but also has excellent charting software. You can customize your chart with dozens of indicators, stock patterns, and chart types. For those wanting to learn more about charts, they have an online "chart school" as well as a daily blog that includes financial analysis.

U.S. Securities and Exchange Commission (SEC)

www.sec.org

The SEC's mission is to protect investors from fraud, insider trader, misleading or false information. They oversee and regulate all market participants, and look for unusual or illegal activity. They make sure that information given to shareholders is legal, and that the markets are fair and orderly. The SEC provides important investor information on their website including the EDGAR database, which includes all the disclosure documents that public companies must file.

Yahoo! Finance
finance.yahoo.com

Yahoo! Finance contains breaking news, stock screeners, simulated portfolios, charts, technical and fundamental indicators, and detailed quotes. The site is easy to use and is loaded with useful information and tools.

About the Author

Michael Sincere interviewed some of the top traders and financial experts in the country to find out the lessons they had learned in the market so he could help others avoid the mistakes he had made. He wrote a book about these lessons, followed by four more books, including *Start Day Trading Now* (Adams Media), *Understanding Options* (McGraw-Hill, 2nd edition), *All About Market Indicators* (McGraw-Hill), and *Understanding Stocks* (McGraw-Hill, 2nd edition).

Sincere has written numerous columns and magazine articles on investing and trading. He has also been interviewed on dozens of national radio programs and has appeared on financial news programs such as CNBC and ABC's *World News Now* to talk about his books.

In addition to being a freelance writer and author, Sincere writes a column for MarketWatch, "Michael Sincere's Long-Term Trader."

You can visit the author's website and blog at *www.michaelsincere.com*. Using indicators and personal observations, each week he writes about the market's next move.

Acknowledgments

Thanks to Earn, my wife, for always being there for me.

I want to thank Peter Archer, my editor at Adams Media, for quickly accepting the book, recognizing its importance, and providing valuable input until it was completed.

Thanks to Mark Wolfinger for making exceptional suggestions and corrections. His encyclopedic knowledge of the stock market was extremely helpful.

To Chip, who created a technical trading system for commodities that was far ahead of its time.

I also want to thank Hazel Garcia for always being an excellent assistant, and web designer Ryan Saunders for creating top-notch websites.

Finally, I want to thank my friends and acquaintances: Lourdes Fernandez-Vidal, Alexandra and Angela Bengtsson, Harvey Small, Sanne Mueller, Karolina Roubickova, Karina Royer, Bob Spector, Bruce Berger, Lucie Stejskalova, Jarle Wirgenes, Lene Wirgenes, Jason Zimmer, Rayna Exelbierd, Evrice Cornelius, Ron Weisberg, Maytee Martinez, Brad Estra, and Jeff Bierman.

Index

How to Contact Me

If you have comments or questions about my book, feel free to send me an e-mail at *msincere@gmail.com*. In addition, if you notice any errors, please let me know so I can make corrections in the next edition. I always enjoy hearing from you.

Finally, if you have time, feel free to stop by my website, *www.michaelsincere.com*. Every week, I use the clues and indicators included in this book to analyze the market.